Brooklyn
Classroom Questions for Comparative Study

A SCENE BY SCENE GUIDE

Amy Farrell

SCENE BY SCENE
WICKLOW, IRELAND

Copyright © 2018 by Scene by Scene.

Without limiting the rights under copyright, this book is sold subject to the condition that it shall not, by way of trade or otherwise be lent, resold, hired out, reproduced, stored on or introduced into a retrieval system, or transmitted, in any form or by any means (electronic, mechanical, photocopying, recording or otherwise), or otherwise circulated, without the publisher's prior consent, in any form other than that in which it is published and without a similar condition, including this condition, being imposed on the subsequent publisher.

All rights reserved. No part of this publication may be recorded or transmitted in any form or by any means electronic, mechanical, photocopying, recording or otherwise without the proper consent of the publisher.

The publisher reserves the right to change, without notice, at any time, the specification of this product, whether by change of materials, colours, format, text revision or any other characteristic.

Scene by Scene
Wicklow, Ireland.
www.scenebyscene.ie

Brooklyn Classroom Questions by Amy Farrell.
ISBN 978-1-910949-74-0

Contents

Part One	2
Cultural Context/Social Setting	4
Literary Genre	10
General Vision and Viewpoint	16
Relationships	21
Hero, Heroine, Villain	25
Part Two	29
Cultural Context/Social Setting	31
Literary Genre	35
General Vision and Viewpoint	38
Relationships	42
Hero, Heroine, Villain	46
Part Three	48
Cultural Context/Social Setting	50
Literary Genre	54
General Vision and Viewpoint	59
Relationships	64
Hero, Heroine, Villain	69
Part Four	72
Cultural Context/Social Setting	74
Literary Genre	77
General Vision and Viewpoint	83

Relationships	87
Hero, Heroine, Villain	91
Part Five	**94**
Cultural Context/Social Setting	95
Literary Genre	99
General Vision and Viewpoint	104
Relationships	110
Hero, Heroine, Villain	115
The Comparative Study	**119**
Cultural Context/Social Setting	120
Literary Genre	125
General Vision and Viewpoint	132
Theme/Issue - Relationships	137
Hero, Heroine, Villain	143
Selecting Key Moments	**146**
The Comparative Study: Comparing Texts	**148**

About This Book

This book is a companion guide for the Comparative Study of *Brooklyn*, directed by John Crowley. Ideally it accompanies a second, detailed viewing and study of the film.

For the purposes of classroom study, I have divided the film into five parts. Each part contains an outline summary, a brief note on Cultural Context/ Social Setting, Literary Genre, General Vision and Viewpoint, Relationships and Hero/Heroine/Villain, and a set of questions on Cultural Context/ Social Setting, Literary Genre, General Vision and Viewpoint, Relationships and Hero/Heroine/Villain. The brief note is intended as a starting point for students, to provide something concrete for each mode that can be developed and built on by exploring the relevant mode-based questions.

Towards the back of the book, there is a short note looking at each mode as a whole, across the entire film, and accompanying questions (please note, there may be some similarity with earlier questions to draw attention to key ideas).

Lastly, there is a section of questions on each mode, designed to prompt comparisons between *Brooklyn* and other Comparative Study texts.

Part One

Summary

From the opening up to 23.25 minutes (Eilis crying in work).

- Eilis walks through dark streets to early mass before going to work in Miss Kelly's shop.

- After work, Eilis tells Miss Kelly she is going to America, and loses her job.

- Eilis has dinner with her sister, Rose, and their mother.

- Eilis and her friend Nancy go to a dance together.

- Rose and Eilis talk as Eilis packs for America.

- Eilis travels to America on a passenger liner. She finds the journey difficult, suffering from sickness, but is befriended by her bunkmate (Georgina) who has been to America before and offers her various pieces of advice.

- Eilis disembarks and passes through immigration control.

- Eilis lives in Mrs Kehoe's boarding house with other Irish women. She begins work at Bartocci's, a fashionable department store, and suffers from homesickness.

Part One
Cultural Context/Social Setting

Eilis' hometown is dull and traditional. The dark streets as the film begins and Eilis yawning to the priest's monotone present this as a drab, predictable world.

Miss Kelly, the shopkeeper, wields a certain power over her customers, serving the well-to-do first and speaking down to her clientele. She seems to feel that her position as shopkeeper and businesswoman gives her the right to treat people this way.

Eilis tells Miss Kelly how a New York priest, Father Flood, has arranged her move to America and sponsored her, organising a job and visa.

Rather than celebrating Eilis' move, Miss Kelly spitefully sacks her and pities Rose, Eilis' sister, who will be left to care for their mother alone.

Eilis feels confined by Enniscorthy. She tells her friend Nancy that with Nancy's beauty, she should be able to choose any man she wants, not hoping that George Sheridan from the rugby club will look her way. Eilis recognises the limitations that living in County Wexford places on their lives and their chance for opportunity.

The dancehall gives an insight into the social scene of this world. Young couples chat and dance stiffly to traditional music.

The boat voyage has its own etiquette and rules, something that Eilis knows nothing of. She does not know which bunk is hers, that the shared toilet is never really shared, or that nobody eats dinner when bad weather is forecast. The boat is a whole new world for Eilis, just as New York will be.

All of Eilis' fellow lodgers at Mrs Kehoe's are Irish girls like her. Mrs Kehoe is a mother-like figure, involving them in dinner conversation and calming their disputes.

Questions

1. How is County Wexford depicted as the film begins? Mention specific details in your answer.

2. When and where does the story begin?

3. What does Eilis going to mass early in the morning like this tell you about this world?

4. Describe Miss Kelly's shop.

5. What is it like, working in Miss Kelly's shop on Sundays? What insight do the scenes in the shop give you into this world?

6. Miss Kelly ignores the waiting customers and has Eilis serve Mrs Brady.
   What is going on here?
   What does this tell you about Miss Kelly, and this place?

7. "Oh mothers are always being left behind in this country." What insight into this world does Miss Kelly's comment give you?

8. Why is Eilis' move to America so significant?
   What will it mean for her and her family?
   How would you feel about making this move, if you were in Eilis' position?

9. Why does Nancy's beauty make Eilis despair of this place? What is Eilis saying about her hometown?

10. How does Eilis describe the boys from the rugby club? What does Eilis' description here tell you about her world?

11. Describe the dance that Eilis and Nancy go to. What does it tell you about this place?

12. What insight do you gain into this world from Eilis' chat with Rose as she packs her belongings?

13. How do Eilis and her family act as she leaves? What does their behaviour here tell you about their society?

14. Comment on the accommodation onboard the ship. How does it impact on the journey?

15. How do you know that the trip to America is a significant event in the lives of these people and their families? Be specific in your answer.

16. "I'll see you later, unless I find a nice man in first to smoke with." Comment on Georgina's (Eilis' bunk mate) attitude towards men.

17. What is the journey like for the passengers?

18. Who has arranged Eilis' move to America?

19. What does Eilis' bunk mate tell her to expect in America?

20. "Sometimes it's nice to talk to people who don't know your auntie."
    In what ways will life in New York be different to life in Enniscorthy?
    Do you expect Eilis to enjoy New York more or less than home?
    Give reasons for your answer.

21. What do you realise about Eilis' clothes when her bunkmate looks through her trunk?

22. What advice does Georgina give Eilis for going through immigration control?
    What does this advice tell you about this world, and Eilis' place in it?

23. What rule is there at dinner in Mrs Kehoe's?

24. What do the women discuss at dinner?
    What does this tell you about their interests?

25. Describe Eilis' job and the place where she works.

26. Describe Eilis' new accommodation.
    Would you like to stay here? Why/why not?

27. What strikes you about Eilis' new life?

28. Is life in New York very different to life at home?
    Use examples to support your view.

29. Do you notice any similarities between home and New York?
Explain your point of view.

30. Does Eilis socialise much or have many friends in New York?

31. Is New York a safe or dangerous place to have moved to, from what you have seen so far?

32. Is family important in this world?
Give reasons for your answer.

33. Is the Church important in this world?
Give reasons for your answer.

34. What factors caused Eilis to emigrate?
Be specific in your answer.

35. Describe the world of Enniscorthy, based on what you have seen so far.

36. Describe the world of New York, based on what you have seen so far.

Part One
Literary Genre

The costumes and hairstyles capture 1950s Ireland. The viewer is instantly aware that this film is set in the past.

County Wexford is presented as a predictable, boring place, and Miss Kelly is a mean, spiteful employer, making it easy to understand why Eilis might want to leave.

Eilis herself appears as a thoughtful, mannerly girl, looking forward to life outside the small world of Enniscorthy. However, her exchanges with her sister, Rose, make us realise that she will miss her family. This move to America is not being taken lightly. It is a big move into the unknown for Eilis, without the familiarity of home or family. From a plot perspective it is a significant move also, as it marks the beginning of Eilis' independent life. Through her move to this new place, and the events that unfold, Eilis will discover who she is.

As Eilis and the other passengers stand on deck, awaiting departure, their uncertainty, sadness and other mixed emotions are clearly seen on their faces. They are journeying into the unknown, with the promise of opportunity, but are leaving behind all that they know. Eilis looks after Rose and her mother as they walk away, wishing, it seems, to still be with them.

Eilis is on her own as she begins the voyage, and her naivity and inexperience show. She does not know the rules of having a cabin, nor does she know to avoid eating when rough seas are forecast. This section shows Eilis' vulnerable character and how daunting it is for her to negotiate her new life.

The difficulties Eilis experiences here make the audience sympathetic to her situation. She is doing her best, without a friend to help her. Her vulnerability makes her easy to relate to and identify with.

The difficulties of the journey may foreshadow certain difficulties that Eilis will have to overcome in New York. There too, there will be a world that Eilis has no experience of, which she will have to learn to negotiate.

Once in New York, Eilis struggles with homesickness, feeling sad and alone in her new job and lodging house. She says little and cries as she reads a letter from home. This is a low point for her, to have travelled so far, to feel so unhappy and alone. Eilis' tears are a visual, emotional sign of her upset, prompting compassion and empathy in the viewer. Seeing Eilis cry, it is easy to understand and identify with how she feels.

Questions

1. What do you notice about the use of colour as the film begins?
   What is the effect of this?
   What is being communicated to the audience?

2. What does Eilis' outfit tell you about the film's setting?

3. What sort of woman is Miss Kelly?
   What is it like, working in her shop?
   Would you like to work for her? Why/why not?

4. What do you learn about Eilis from seeing her work in Miss Kelly's shop?

5. What do you learn about these characters and this place from the film's opening sequence?
   Be specific in your answer.

6. What has made it possible for Eilis to go to America?

7. Is going to America a daunting prospect?
   Give reasons for your answer.

8. What are your first impressions of Eilis' mother and her sister, Rose?

9. Describe the dance Eilis and Nancy go to.
   Is it an exciting event?
   What does it add to the story?

10. Do you see a different side to Eilis when she is with Nancy?
    Why is this the case?
    How does this add to your understanding of her character?

11. Does Eilis enjoy the dance, do you think?
    What insight does this give you into her character?

12. What does Eilis' decision to go to America tell you about her character?
    Does it weigh on Eilis' mother and sister, or do they support this move?
    Give reasons for your answer.

13. Is Eilis leaving Ireland a significant plot point?
    Give reasons for your answer.

14. Comment on the imagery as Eilis stands on deck preparing for departure.

15. What makes Eilis' departure dramatic and emotional?
    Pinpoint how emotion is created in this scene.
    How does the soundtrack add to this moment?

16. How do you get a sense of Eilis' character during the voyage?
    Mention specific details that show you the type of person she is.

17. Does the scene where Eilis is sick and locked out of the toilet make you laugh, or do you feel sorry for her?
Give reasons for your answer.

18. How does Eilis' bunkmate (Georgina) treat her after she is sick?
What does Eilis' bunkmate do when she hears the other cabin locked Eilis out of the toilet all night?
How do these details create a sense of her character for you?

19. Comment on the image of Eilis walking through the backlit door out of immigration.
How does this image add to the story?

20. How does Eilis react to hearing that letters arrived for her from home?
What insight does this give you into how she is feeling?

21. Why do we see Eilis reading her letters in so many places?
What is being communicated to the audience?

22. Is Eilis settling in well to her new job and home?
What effect does this have on the audience?

23. What are your impresssions of these characters after watching Part One?

24. What strikes you about Eilis after watching Part One?
Be specific in your answer.

25. Is Eilis a vulnerable character, in your view?
Does this make her easy to identify with and relate to?
Give reasons for your answer.

26. Is Eilis a weak or brave character in your opinion?
Use examples to support your point of view.

27. What age is Eilis, do you think?
Give reasons for your answer.
Is she a typical example of someone this age?
Explain your point of view.

28. How important is the soundtrack in telling this story?
Use examples to support your point of view.

29. What interests you in this story so far?
Be specific in your answer.

Part One
General Vision and Viewpoint

County Wexford is presented as boring and predictable, and Miss Kelly is a difficult, demanding, spiteful employer. We realise quickly that there is not much potential for excitement or growth in a place like this.

At dinner, Rose trails off while saying how long Eilis will be in America for. Eilis is perhaps leaving forever, going into the unknown and leaving her family behind, which is a daunting prospect.

The dance shows the limits and limitations of Eilis' world and her life if she stays in Enniscorthy. She hopes for more than a dance with one of the rugby club boys, she wants more from life. The staid social scene here helps to explain her outlook and why she feels America is the best choice for her.

Eilis' chat with Rose, though upsetting for them both, shows Rose's belief that opportunity lies in America for Eilis. Rose thinks there is not enough in Enniscorthy for Eilis, and that she must travel to make a future for herself. Though saddened by their parting, there is a selflessness and optimism in Rose's plans and hopes for her sister that is very positive.

As Eilis stands onboard, ready for departure, there is sadness as she leaves her family, particularly her sister. However, the journey ahead is the path to Eilis' future. It is a bittersweet moment, both sad and hopeful at once.

This journey to America has uncertain, problematic beginnings. Eilis naively eats a full dinner and is locked out of the toilet by fellow passengers when she is violently ill. This shows how cold-hearted strangers can be, introducing doubt about whether inexperienced Eilis has made a mistake in her decision to emigrate.

However, her bunkmate's kindness and advice after this shows the warmth and kindness of strangers. Eilis is not alone for long, a positive note to the journey.

Also, her bunkmate's comments about how well set-up she is, and how she will meet people easily enough, are encouraging. This move is daunting for Eilis, but her new found ally points out the positives to her in an optimistic, forward-looking way.

Eilis is lonely and homesick at first in New York. She speaks little and is unsure of herself in this new city. Her loneliness and homesickness make her unhappy, this is a sad and difficult time for Eilis.

Questions

1. How does Miss Kelly treat the customers in her shop?
   Why does she treat them this way?
   What does this suggest about her outlook?
   What is the director suggesting about human nature here?

2. How does Eilis feel about Miss Kelly's behaviour?
   What stops her from saying something?
   How does this make you feel?

3. How does Miss Kelly react to Eilis' news of going to America?
   What does this tell you about the type of person that she is?

4. Eilis' move to America will be permanent.
   What problems will this create for her and her family?
   How must they be feeling about this move?

5. Does Eilis like living in County Wexford, do you think?
   How does she view the place?
   Be specific in your answer.

6. Why doesn't Eilis make more of an effort with her dress for her night out with Nancy?
   What does this suggest about her outlook?

7. "I can't buy you the kind of life you need."
   Why must Eilis go to America, according to her sister?

Describe Rose's outlook here.
Do you agree with Rose's view of things?

8. How do you feel as Eilis stands onboard and blows her sister a kiss?
How must she be feeling?
Comment on the mood at this point.

9. Is Eilis selfish to leave her family like this?
Is it necessary sometimes, to be selfish, in order to succeed in life?
Explain your point of view.

10. What does the way Eilis is treated by her fellow passengers suggest about life?

11. "Please unlock it."
Do you feel sorry for Eilis as she makes her way to America?
Give reasons for your answer.

12. Is Eilis supported or isolated in her move to America?
What does this suggest about the writer's view of life?

13. What effect does talking with her bunkmate about America have on Eilis?
How would you feel, if you were her?

14. Eilis walks out of immigration control and through a door into bright light.
How does this image affect the mood at this point?

Do you think she will enjoy her new life in America?
Give reasons for your answer.

15. How well does Eilis settle in to life in New York?
Is she happy? Give reasons for your answer.

16. Is Eilis welcomed and accepted in New York?

17. How do Mrs Kehoe and her lodgers and Eilis' new employer treat her?
What does this tell you about people?
What does this tell you about life?
Is this a positive or negative worldview?
Explain your point of view.

18. Do you think Eilis' move to Brooklyn is for the best?
Fully explain your point of view, mentioning the positives and negatives to this move.

Part One
Relationships

Miss Kelly speaks sharply to Eilis when she asks to talk to her later. When she hears Eilis is leaving for America, she tells her not to come back to work, and pities Eilis' sister, Rose, who will have to care for their mother. Miss Kelly is spiteful, intentionally hurting Eilis here.

As Eilis has dinner with Rose and her mother, it is clear that the sisters have a close bond, sharing looks and glances rather than having to say anything aloud. However, this practice of leaving things unsaid could suggest that true feelings and emotions are often concealed and suppressed in their home.

Eilis and Nancy are good friends, with Eilis thinking the world of Nancy. Eilis thinks her friend should have her pick of men, rather than having to wait for George Sheridan to ask her to dance.

Eilis' chat with Rose as she packs gives an insight into their relationship. Rose, though sad to see her go, believes there is a better life, with more opportunity, for Eilis in New York. She truly wants what is best for her sister.

They do not discuss the possibility of not seeing each other again. Eilis tries to express how sad that would make her, but Rose changes topic, not wanting to discuss it. Once again, feelings are pushed down and things are left unsaid.

The sisters care about each other and will miss each other terribly. However, both know that Eilis' move is the best thing for her, and so Rose completely supports her in her move abroad.

The closeness of Eilis and Rose's bond is seen as Eilis stands on deck, holding her sister's gaze for as long as she can before departing. This move is difficult for Eilis, but she and her sister believe it is the right thing for her to do. They are putting aside their own feelings, to make sure that Eilis has a bright future.

At first, Eilis is isolated and alone as she begins her journey, without anyone to look out for her. However, after her first night of illness, her bunkmate Georgina takes her under her wing, offering friendship and advice for the journey.

Eilis is thinking of her family at home, asking Georgina how long it takes for letters from Ireland to arrive. These thoughts of family and home continue when she arrives in New York. Eilis does little to make new friends at first, her thoughts are of home, and she is very sad and homesick.

Questions

1. How does Miss Kelly speak to Eilis as she unlocks the shop?

2. How does Miss Kelly react to Eilis' news that she is "away to America"?
   Is she supportive of Eilis' move?

3. What will become of Eilis' sister, Rose, when Eilis leaves, according to Miss Kelly?
   What insight does this give you into Eilis' family?

4. Describe the dinner scene with Eilis, Rose and their mother.
   How do they get on?

5. How will Eilis moving to America impact on her relationships with her family?

6. Are Eilis and Nancy good friends?
   Give reasons for your answer.

7. What makes Rose say that she should have looked after Eilis better?
   How does Rose feel about Eilis, do you think?

8. Why don't the sisters discuss the possibility of not seeing each other again?
   What does this tell you about their relationship?
   Do they tell each other how they feel here?
   Why/why not?

9. How do Eilis and her family behave as she departs?
   How does this make you feel?

10. Does Eilis get on well with her bunkmate?
    Use examples to support the points you make.

11. Eilis asks her bunkmate how long it takes for letters from Ireland to arrive in New York.
    What does this tell you?

12. How does Eilis' bunkmate help her during the voyage?
    Does she treat her with kindness or contempt?

13. How well do the women in Mrs Kehoe's get on on with one another?

14. Explain the relationship dynamic in Mrs Kehoe's.

15. How does Eilis' manager treat her?
    Use examples to support your view.

16. "She's that sort."
    How do the other girls at Mrs Kehoe's view Eilis?

17. How does Eilis respond to reading Rose's letter?
    What does this tell you about how she is feeling?

18. Is Eilis very isolated in New York?
    Explain your point of view.

19. From what you have seen so far, what are your impressions of Eilis' relationships with her family?

Part One
Hero, Heroine, Villain

Eilis appears at first to be polite, quiet and respectful, aware of the need to get along with Miss Kelly. She is nervous about telling her employer about her plans to go to America, and with good reason, as Miss Kelly spitefully sacks her, and draws attention to Eilis' sister, Rose, being left to care for their mother.

Eilis is more talkative and outspoken when she goes out with her friend Nancy. Her chat here shows how closed in and confined she finds the routine of life in County Wexford to be.

Eilis is a good friend, assuring Nancy that George Sheridan, the young man she is interested in, will ask her to dance.

Eilis is sad to be leaving home, particularly her sister Rose, but she realises that there is not much for her at home. She bravely makes this move to America, knowing that it will not be easy.

Eilis is unsure of herself on the trip to America, having never made a journey like this before. She is the only guest at dinner on the first evening, showing her inexperience, and she is violently ill her first night at sea.

Her bunkmate looks after her after this, offering her advice and telling her about New York. This makes us realise how naive and inexperienced Eilis is.

She is very homesick at first. Everything is strange and unfamiliar, and Eilis longs for home. Letters from her family make her cry, as she struggles to be away from them.

Questions

1. How does Eilis feel about skipping the queue for Mrs Brady?
   What does this tell you about her?
   Why does she do as Miss Kelly tells her?
   What does this tell you about her?

2. What does Eilis think of George Sheridan (the man her friend Nancy is interested in)?
   What do her feelings here tell you about her?

3. Is Eilis a good friend to Nancy?
   Give reasons for your answer.

4. Eilis is the only passenger to eat dinner on the first day of the voyage.
   What does this tell you about her?

5. How is Eilis' youth and lack of experience seen on the boat journey to America?

6. What insight into Eilis' character do you gain from her conversations with her bunkmate?

7. Does Eilis want to go to America, do you think?
   Explain your point of view.

8. How is Eilis affected by homesickness?

9. Is Eilis brave to go to America?
   Explain your point of view.

10. Is Eilis a vulnerable character?
    Does this make you like her more or less?
    Give a reason for your answer.

11. Is Eilis a weak character?
    Explain your point of view fully.

12. Based on what you have seen so far, what age, do you think, is Eilis?
    Give reasons for your answer.
    Is she naive or wise for her age?
    Give reasons for your answer.

13. What are your first impressions of Eilis?
    Give reasons for your answer.

Part Two

Summary

From 23.25 minutes (Eilis crying in work) up to 43.25 minutes (Rose sitting by the river).

- Father Flood comes at once to comfort Eilis and help her deal with her homesickness. He has enrolled her in book-keeping night classes.

- Eilis goes to her first night class and enjoys it.

- Eilis helps out at Father Flood's Christmas dinner for the old Irish men of New York.

- Mrs Kehoe invites Eilis in for a drink on Christmas evening.

- Eilis goes to a dance and meets Tony. He walks her home and asks for a date the following weekend.

- Tony eagerly listens to everything Eilis says on their date.

- Mrs Kehoe's lodgers are keen to hear all about Tony.

- Tony waits outside Eilis' college so that he can see her. He asks her to have dinner with his family.

- Rose reads a letter from Eilis, smiling and crying.

Part Two
Cultural Context/Social Setting

Eilis works in a large department store, where her manager is abrupt and to the point, but also watches out for her, fetching Father Flood when she suffers from homesickness. This is a new world, full of strangers, but it is not a cold or unfeeling place, just an unfamiliar one.

Father Flood comforts and reassures Eilis, and also offers her an opportunity, in the form of a book-keeping night class. His surprise at her lack of a 'proper' job at home highlights the lack of opportunity in Ireland for a young woman like Eilis. Her enrollment in a night class shows the possibility for her to improve her life and advance in America, if she is willing to work hard and study.

It is interesting that Eilis' classmates are all men. She is entering a male dominated world by studying like this. However, no one passes any remark on her presence. Although a female student may be unusual, there is nothing to stop her from studying like this.

The dance Eilis attends with Dolores is similar to the dances at home. This social scene, coupled with her Irish housemates, shows how her circle of experience has not broadened immediately upon arriving in America. Eilis is still an Irish girl, surrounded by Irish girls.

Eilis meets Tony, a young Italian man, at the Irish dance, and he walks her home, showing the traditional values of the time.

Questions

1. How does Eilis' manager, Miss Fortini, deal with her homesickness?
   How does she treat her here?

2. What surprised Father Flood about Eilis?
   What difference does this highlight between County Wexford and New York?

3. From what you have seen so far, how important is the Church in these characters' lives?
   Include examples to explain your view.

4. What do you notice about those attending Eilis' night class?
   What does this suggest about this world?

5. How does Eilis spend Christmas?
   What insight does this give you into life for the Irish in New York?

6. Why does Mrs Kehoe give Eilis the basement room?
   What insight does Mrs Kehoe provide into the place of women in society here?

7. Describe the dance that Eilis goes to.
   Is it very different to the dance at home in Ireland?
   Why is this the case?

8. "I'd love to meet a fella."
   What does Dolores' attitude tell you about this world?

9. Why does Tony tell Eilis that he is not Irish?
   Why is this significant to him?
   What does it tell you about this world?

10. Is there anything old-fashioned or formal in Eilis' developing relationship with Tony?
    Use examples to support your view.

11. Why, do you think, is inviting Eilis to dinner with his family so important to Tony?
    What does it tell you about his values and his world?

12. What question does Miss Fortini, Eilis' manager, ask about Tony?
    What insight does this give you into their world?

13. Is Eilis and Tony's blossoming relationship similar to or different from a new relationship today?
    Be specific in your answer.
    What does this tell you about their world?

14. Is life in New York very different to life at home in Ireland?
    What strikes you about each of these places?
    Use examples to support the points that you make.

Part Two
Literary Genre

Father Flood's visit and Eilis' enrollment in a night class reminds the viewer that there are opportunities for Eilis in New York. Although she is finding it difficult now, and is lonely and isolated, Father Flood reminds us that this city has great potential to offer her.

Christmas Day at Father Flood's dinner shows that New York can be lonely for many. These men have built America, and are now largely forgotten. This episode adds to the nostalgic mood of missing home.

The dance Eilis goes to with Dolores is boring at first, until Eilis dances with Tony. He is entranced by her from the moment he sees her. They get on well together, and Tony walks her home, asking if he can see her next week. This is a significant development, as their romance introduces a love story into the plot and brightens the mood through Eilis' happiness.

Questions

1. How does Eilis attending night classes add to your understanding of her character?
   What does it tell you about her?

2. What does the Christmas lunch, and Frankie's song in particular, add to the story?

3. Does Eilis enjoy the dance that she goes to with Dolores? What does this add to the story?

4. How does Eilis treat Dolores at the dance?
   What does this add to your understanding of her character?

5. What are your first impressions of Tony, the young Italian man who asks Eilis to dance?

6. How do the other girls from Mrs Kehoe's react to seeing Eilis leave with Tony?
   What does this add to the story?

7. What do you learn about Eilis' character from her date with Tony?
   Is he interested in going out with her again, do you think?
   How does this development add to the story?
   Explain your point of view.

8. Do you expect something serious to develop between Eilis and Tony?
   Give reasons for your answer.

9. What strikes you about Tony's character?
    Be specific in your answer.

10. How has the mood of the film changed since Eilis met Tony?

11. "Eilis, you're like a different person."
    Explain the change you see in Eilis.

12. What does Eilis practising with spaghetti add to the story?
    What does it tell you about her relationship with Tony?

13. How does seeing Rose read Eilis' letter add to the story?
    How does it make you feel?

14. Is Eilis and Tony's developing relationship shown to be very romantic?
    Give reasons for your answer.

15. How is the innocence and optimism of Tony and Eilis communicated in this section?

16. Is Eilis a character that you like or can relate to?
    Give reasons for your answer.

Part Two
General Vision and Viewpoint

Eilis' manager shows compassion and understanding in sending for Father Flood when she sees that Eilis is upset. This is a quiet act of kindness, she gives Eilis time to compose herself and fetches someone who will make her feel better.

Eilis' chat with Father Flood shows how choosing what is best can be sad and lonely at times. Eilis is homesick, missing her sister especially. Father Flood's kind words shows the goodness of people.

Additionally, his enrollment of Eilis in a night class shows the potential and possibility of New York. Here, her hard work may earn her a successful career, if she perseveres through this tough time, she will be rewarded for it. The writer suggests that Eilis' struggles and sadness will be overcome and that she will be rewarded for her hardships, a positive and optimistic outlook.

Eilis is much happier once she meets Tony. She smiles and talks more, and has fun with him. Now that she has found him, her homesickness and loneliness are no longer a problem. With Tony, she enjoys talking about her life, instead of missing home.

Rose reads a letter from Eilis by the river. It makes her smile, and cry, to read of her sister's new life in New York. Rose misses Eilis, but is happy to hear that she is happy, and that she has a boyfriend. There is genuine warmth and kindness in Rose's sadness that Eilis is gone, and in the way she wants the best for her sister. However, it is sad that while Eilis has found new happiness, Rose is left at home bearing her sadness alone. Thus Eilis' happiness is also tinged with sadness for the viewer, who is keenly aware of Rose at home, without her.

Questions

1. How is Eilis feeling?
   What advice does Father Flood offer about homesickness?
   Is this a positive or negative outlook?

2. What does the Christmas dinner for the Irish men make you realise?

3. What is the atmosphere like as Eilis walks home in the falling snow?

4. How is Dolores, the new girl, treated by Mrs Kehoe's other girls?
   How does this make you feel?
   Do you feel sorry for Dolores?

5. Does Eilis have a good time at the dance?
   How, do you think, will things develop between Eilis and Tony?
   Is this a positive development for Eilis?
   Give reasons for your answer.

6. Does Eilis and Tony's date go well?
   Do they have a good time?

7. Does Eilis having a boyfriend improve things in Mrs Kehoe's?
   Why/why not?
   Why, do you think, is this the case?

8. Tony waits outside her nightclass, so that he can see Eilis. How does this make you feel?

9. Rose laughs and cries as she reads Eilis' letter.
What does this tell you about how she feels?
What does this tell you about Rose's life?
How does this make you feel?

10. Has Rose made sacrifices for Eilis?
Explain your point of view.

11. Is Eilis overwhelmed by her move to Brooklyn?
Is she coping well?
What does this suggest about life?

12. Is Eilis dating Tony a positive or negative development?
Give reasons for your answer.

Part Two
Relationships

Father Flood is very kind to Eilis, enrolling her in night classes, providing both a distraction and a way for her to unlock her potential. He shows a good understanding of people, and of what it is like to be a stranger in a new place.

Mrs Kehoe gives Eilis the best room in her house, rewarding her as she thinks highly of her.

The lodgers are mean to Dolores, the new girl, making jokes at her expense. Eilis behaves more kindly towards her, and takes her to the dance, but tires of her, and leaves her on her own.

Eilis and Tony get on well from the start, dancing, and then walking home together. They go out for dinner and Eilis hardly eats anything, she is so busy chatting. She is comfortable and happy with Tony, it is a very positive relationship.

Tony waits for her outside night class so that he can spend time with her on her journey home, a sweet and romantic gesture. He invites her to dinner with his family, keen for them to meet her. They smile a lot together, and appear as a young couple, in love.

Eilis writes to Rose, telling her all about Tony and how being with him has helped her be less homesick.

Rose smiles as she reads, but cries too. She is happy for her sister, but also suffers from missing her.

Questions

1. What does Eilis' manager do when Eilis starts crying in work?
   Comment on how she treats her here.

2. Is Eilis very isolated in New York?
   Explain your point of view.

3. How does Father Flood treat Eilis?

4. Why is Father Flood helping Eilis?

5. How does Mrs Kehoe treat Eilis?
   Include examples to support the points that you make.

6. "Will the other girls not mind?"
   What strikes you about the group of girls living in Mrs Kehoe's and the way they get along together?

7. How do the girls treat Dolores, the new girl?

8. Does Eilis get on well with Tony when she first meets him?
   Are they relaxed and comfortable together?
   Explain your point of view.

9. Are you surprised that Tony asks Eilis out?
   What makes you say this?

10. Does Eilis' date with Tony go well?

11. How does the dynamic at dinner in Mrs Kehoe's change once Eilis starts dating Tony?

12. Does Mrs Kehoe get on well with her lodgers?
    Explain your point of view.

13. Tony waits outside Eilis' night class so that he can see her. What does this tell you about how he feels about her?

14. "I'll sign up for two movies".
    Describe Eilis and Tony's relationship at this point.

15. How much does Eilis tell her sister about life in New York?
    What does this tell you about her relationship with Rose?

16. How does Rose respond to reading Eilis' letter?
    Why does she respond this way?

17. Is Eilis happier, do you think, since she started going out with Tony?
    What does this tell you about their relationship?

18. Do Eilis and Tony make a good couple, do you think?
    Give reasons for your answer.

Part Two
Hero, Heroine, Villain

Eilis, although very sad and missing home, follows Father Flood's advice and attends night classes. She shows resilience and determination, continuing to try to adjust to her new life rather than giving up.

She enjoys the book-keeping class, showing she is interested, eager to learn and bright.

Eilis helps out at Father Flood's Christmas Day dinner, something the other lodgers at Mrs Kehoe's avoid. This shows her dutiful nature, but also her kindness and generosity.

Eilis' kindness is also the reason why she takes Dolores, the new lodger, to the Irish dance, even though she thinks Dolores is awful. However, she leaves Dolores when two of the other girls arrive, and walks home with Tony, showing that she is not merely a dutiful doormat to be depended on.

Eilis chats freely and openly with Tony. She is not shy or self-conscious at all, and has fun with him.

Questions

1. Is Eilis open and honest with Father Flood?

2. Does Eilis enjoy her night class?
   What makes you say this?

3. Why does Eilis help Father Flood on Christmas Day?
   What does this tell you about her?

4. How does Eilis treat Dolores, the new girl in Mrs Kehoe's?
   What does this tell you about Eilis?

5. Why does Eilis let Tony walk her home?

6. The other girls in Mrs Kehoe's say that Eilis won't say anything about having found herself a new man.
   Why doesn't Eilis tell them all about Tony, do you think?
   What does this tell you about Eilis' personality?

7. Eilis practises eating spaghetti before going to dinner at Tony's.
   What does this tell you about her?

8. Does Eilis like Tony, do you think?
   Give reasons for your answer.

9. Is Eilis settling in to life in New York?
   Explain your point of view.

Part Three

Summary

From 43.26 minutes (Eilis and Tony walking upstairs) up to 1.05.33 minutes (Eilis and Tony in bed).

- Eilis goes to dinner in Tony's house with his parents and brothers.
- After walking Eilis home, Tony tells Eilis that he loves her.
- Eilis asks Sheila questions about marriage.
- Tony meets Eilis after night class and she tells him she feels the same way about him.
- Eilis brings Father Flood the good news of success in her exams.
- Eilis and Tony go to the beach at Coney Island.
- Eilis' mother discovers Rose's body. Father Flood breaks the news to Eilis.

- Tony takes Eilis to Long Island, to show her the site of their future home, should she want it.

- Eilis arrives at Tony's in the middle of the night, telling him she has to go home to her mother in Ireland. He proposes marriage and they have sex.

Part Three
Cultural Context/Social Setting

Tony's mother is impressed that Eilis can eat pasta properly, and that she is going to night classes. Their family meal together is relaxed and friendly, Tony's family are chatty and welcoming, even his little brother, who does not like Irish people.

This dinner shows how important family is in this world, and how important it is for Tony that his family should meet and like Eilis.

Frankie's comments touch on racial prejudice, but it is a minor episode, keeping any issue of racism in the background.

After walking her home, Tony tells Eilis that he loves her. There is a youthful hopefulness and openness in him that speaks of a certain innocence in his generation. There is a sense that he and Eilis are part of a romantic, youthful age, that wholeheartedly believes in love and romance.

Eilis asks Sheila why she is not married. It seems that to be a single woman in this world is unusual. Sheila tells Eilis that her husband left her after meeting somebody else. Eilis asks her if she would marry again, realising that this is where her relationship with Tony is heading.

Sheila says she would marry again, to have her own home rather than the boarding house. Marriage represents a certain stability and surety for her, even though she imagines her future husband as a bad-tempered man. Marriage is what all of these women seek; it is expected of, and by them.

Much is made of organising a swimsuit for Eilis, so that Tony will find her attractive when they go to the beach. This is an attitude that Mrs Kehoe's household and Eilis' manager, Miss Fortini, share.

Father Flood is tasked with breaking the news of Rose's death to Eilis. Eilis' distance from home, and the separateness of her new world is highlighted here. Because she is so far away, Eilis misses her sister's funeral.

Eilis feels a duty to return home to Ireland out of responsibility to her mother.

Tony proposes to Eilis, wanting to secretly marry her before she leaves. When she agrees, they go to Eilis' room and have sex. It seems that the marriage proposal is necessary in this world, to give them licence to be together intimately. Also, Tony must feel that this formal bond will ensure that Eilis returns to New York, showing the significance and importance of marriage vows in this world. Despite the romance of their relationship, he may secretly fear that once she goes home, she may not return. We are reminded that Eilis has two separate, parallel worlds to negotiate.

Questions

1. What does Frankie do at dinner that gets him into trouble?
   What does this reveal to you about this world?

2. Is family important in the world of *Brooklyn*?
   Give reasons for your answer.

3. Does Tony's mother like Eilis, do you think?
   Why is this the case?
   What insight does this give you into this world?

4. What is important to Tony's family, based on what you learn of them at dinner?

5. What does Eilis' dinner with Tony's family show you about this world?

6. Tony walks Eilis home, hugs her, and tells her that he loves her.
   What does this tell you about society in the film and the way relationships work?

7. What does Eilis ask Sheila?
   What do her questions, and Sheila's answers, tell you about marriage in this world?

8. Why, do you think, does Eilis want to be with Tony?
   What does this reveal to you about this world?

9. How do the other girls react to the news of Eilis' trip to Coney Island?
   What does this tell you about this world?

10. According to Mrs Kehoe, why must Eilis think carefully about her swimming costume?
    Comment on her attitude here.

11. What does the scene where Eilis tries on a bathing suit tell you about how women are viewed in this world?

12. We see Eilis and Tony kissing in the sea.
    Is their relationship developing quickly or slowly, in your view?
    Can you explain why this is the case?
    Would this be unusual today? Explain your point of view.

13. Who breaks the news of Rose's death to Eilis?
    Why have they been given this task?

14. Tony takes Eilis to the site of their future home and tells her his business plans.
    What is he offering her?
    Is America presented as the land of opportunity, do you think?
    Give reasons for your answer.

15. Eilis agrees to marry Tony and they go to her room and have sex.
    Explain why the marriage proposal was necessary here.

Part Three
Literary Genre

The mood at dinner in Tony's is relaxed and welcoming. Tony is eager for things to go well between Eilis and his family. After walking her home, Tony tells Eilis that he loves her. This intensifies the love story as their relationship develops. Eilis does not reply in kind to Tony. This adds a note of doubt and tension to the storyline.

Later, Eilis asks Sheila questions about marriage, suggesting that she feels uncertain about it. Asking Sheila also reminds the audience that Eilis is away from home, without friends or family to turn to for advice.

It is a touching moment when Eilis tells Tony that she feels the same way about him. He is overjoyed, thinking that Eilis wanted to break up with him. He appears as a happy, loving character.

Eilis and Tony's relationship becomes more serious. This is clear when they kiss in the water at Coney Island, demonstrating that their relationship is becoming more demonstrative and physical.

Eilis narrates a letter to her sister, mentioning her hopes of visiting home, as her mother discovers Rose's body on-screen. This is a very shocking moment in the story, abruptly changing the mood. Eilis' happiness with Tony is replaced with loss, sadness and grief.

Rose's death is significant from a plot perspective. Eilis' mother is now grieving alone in Ireland, without family to turn to for support. This will weigh heavily on Eilis and make her feel like she must return home.

Tony comforts Eilis, showing his kind, caring character. When Eilis says she is going home, he proposes that they secretly marry. Eilis is reluctant, but he presses the issue, and she agrees. This secret marriage, prompted by Eilis' return home, will cement their relationship, and in Tony's eyes, ensure Eilis' return to New York.

The sex scene in Eilis' basement apartment is more uncomfortable than romantic. It shows their commitment to one another, now that they are to be married.

There is tension and uncertainty now Rose's death has dramatically changed the course of events, making the story's outcome unpredictable.

Questions

1. Is dinner with Tony's family a tense affair?

2. Why does this dinner matter so much to Tony?
   How does it affect the storyline?

3. Does Eilis make a good impression on Tony's family?
   Give reasons for your answer.

4. Tony walks Eilis home and tells her that he loves her.
   Is Tony a very innocent and romantic character, do you think?
   What does he add to your understanding of the film's setting?

5. Eilis asks Sheila questions about marriage.
   What does this tell you about Eilis?
   How does this add to the story?

6. How is tension built around Eilis' conversation with Tony after night class?

7. Are Eilis and Tony a realistic young couple?
   Give reasons for your answer.
   Are Eilis and Tony a relatable young couple?
   Give reasons for your answer.
   Are Eilis and Tony a likeable young couple?
   Give reasons for your answer.

8. What is Rose's letter about?
   What is the effect of this letter, at this point?

9. Comment on Eilis' outfit and the time of year as Eilis goes to visit Father Flood.
   What is being communicated visually here?

10. What does Eilis and Tony's trip to Coney Island add to the story?
    Be specific in your answer.

11. Comment on the image of Eilis and Tony kissing in the sea.
    What is being communicated to the audience?

12. What is the effect of hearing Eilis' letter as her mother discovers Rose's body?

13. What is the mood like as Father Flood tells Eilis of her sister's death?
    Is this a very emotional scene? Why/why not?
    Comment on the use of colour here and what it adds to the scene.

14. How does Eilis' phone conversation with her mother make you feel?
    What is her mother asking her to do?

15. What is the impact of Rose's death on the storyline?
    How does it complicate things for Eilis?

16. How does Tony feel about Eilis going home?
    Is he understanding or selfish here?

17. Why do we see Eilis imagining her mother in church?

18. Why, do you think, does Tony propose?
    What is his motivation here?
    Is he being loving or manipulative?
    Is this an exciting or tense moment?
    Explain your view.
    Is this a romantic moment?
    Explain your view.

19. Is the sex scene romantic?
    What is being communicated to the audience here?

20. What problems do you anticipate for Eilis?
    Use examples to support your view.

21. Is this an exciting moment in the story?
    Give reasons for your answer.

Part Three
General Vision and Viewpoint

Eilis and Tony's relationship is very loving and positive. He mentions their future children, imagining their life together. When Eilis tells Tony she feels the same way about him, he is overjoyed. There is happiness and warmth in this relationship that is very positive, adding to an optimistic general vision and viewpoint at this point.

Eilis passes her exams and Father Flood comments on how changed she is from the miserable girl who wanted to go home. Her outlook has changed completely and she is now making a good life for herself in New York.

The news of Rose's death comes as a devastating blow for Eilis. Her separateness and the distance from home is emphasised here, she will not be able to go to Rose's funeral. Her mother's phonecall underlines Eilis' grief and upset, each feeling very sad and alone. Rose's death completely changes the film's outlook, changing from a happy, bright outlook, to one focused on death and sadness.

Tony comforts Eilis in her grief, understanding her need to go home, but he is also fearful that she won't come back. The security of their world has been compromised, Rose's death shows that nothing is certain.

Tony takes Eilis to Long Island, to show her the site of their future home. At this time of great sadness, Tony offers Eilis a home, a gesture that is loving, forward-looking and optimistic.

When Eilis says she has to go home to her mother, Tony proposes, wanting to make sure that Eilis will come back to him. Once she agrees to marriage, they have sex, further developing their relationship. Tony wants their bond to be strong, to ensure Eilis' return. He is looking to the future, past Eilis' current need to go home.

However, perhaps Tony is manipulative here, rushing Eilis to marry him so that he can get the guarantee of her return that he craves. He thinks of himself, during this very difficult time for Eilis, and this negatively impacts on the general vision and viewpoint.

Questions

1. Tony tells Eilis that he loves her.
   How does this make you feel?

2. How does Eilis respond to Tony's declaration of love?
   Why, do you think, does she respond this way?
   How does this make you feel?

3. Is Eilis and Tony's developing relationship a positive or negative portrayal of relationships?
   Give reasons for your answer.

4. How does Sheila, Eilis' fellow lodger, imagine her future husband?
   What does this tell you about her life?
   How does this make you feel?

5. What does Eilis tell Tony when she meets him after night class?
   How does this make you feel?
   What kind of development is this?

6. What is the tone of Rose's letter?

7. How is Rose feeling without Eilis?
   How does this make you feel?

8. "Qualifications and a boyfriend Eilis. You're not the miserable young girl who wanted to go home last winter."
   How is life for Eilis these days?

What sort of future lies ahead of her?
Is this a positive or negative future life?

9. "I think perhaps she was ill, and she knew she was ill, and she didn't tell anybody."
Why, do you think, did Rose keep her illness a secret?
How does this make you feel?
What does it suggest about the life Rose was living?

10. "I'll never see her again."
How does Father Flood comfort Eilis?
Does he make her feel better?

11. What is the impact of Rose's death on Eilis?
How does this make you feel?

12. How does Tony feel about Eilis going home?
Does he trust her?
Do you understand how he is feeling here?

13. Why does Tony take Eilis to Long Island?
What is he offering her?
Is this a positive or controlling gesture?
What is your response to his offer?

14. Is Tony's marriage proposal romantic or manipulative?
Explain your view.
Would Eilis be happy with Tony, in your opinion?

15. Comment on the circumstances of Rose's death.
How does this impact on the general vision and viewpoint?

16. What does Rose's death remind us about life?

17. What is the mood like, at this point in the story?
    Give reasons for your answer.

18. Why does Tony propose to Eilis, in your view?
    How does this affect the general vision and viewpoint?
    Be specific in your answer.

19. How has Rose's death changed the mood and outlook of the story?
    Be specific in your answer.

Part Three
Relationships

The dinner at Tony's shows how much Tony wants to pursue this relationship with Eilis. It is important to him that Eilis and his family get on well. At dinner he makes a comment about their future children, showing how he imagines a future for him and Eilis.

After walking her home, Tony tells Eilis that he loves her. She replies by thanking him for the evening. She is more cautious than Tony, who is open and enthusiastic about his feelings for her.

She thinks about marriage before telling Tony the following night that she feels the same way.

Their relationship is developing and becoming more serious. At Coney Island they appear as a young couple in love, kissing passionately in the sea.

When Eilis hears the devastating news of her sister's death, it is Tony that she turns to for comfort and support.

Rose's death brings Eilis' family bonds to the fore. She feels a sense of duty and responsibility to go and be with her mother at this sad time.

Fearing perhaps that Eilis will not return from Ireland, Tony shows her the site of their future home and proposes that they secretly marry. He does not want to lose her, but Eilis wonders whether he trusts her to return. He pushes the issue, wanting to be married before she leaves. She agrees and they spend the night together. This physical development in their relationship is perhaps a gesture of the commitment they feel to one another.

Tony is clearly very much in love with Eilis, but this question of doubt remains. He is not happy for Eilis to go home without marrying him first. This need for a legal, binding dimension to their commitment, may suggest he doubts how Eilis truly feels about him.

Questions

1. Why does Tony warn Eilis about his brother, Frankie?
   What does this tell you about how Tony feels about Eilis?

2. Tony's brothers are surprised that he has not mentioned baseball to Eilis before now.
   Can you suggest why this is the case?

3. Tony says, "If our kids end up supporting the Yankees or the Giants it would break my heart."
   How does Eilis react to his words?
   Why is this the case, do you think?

4. Tony tells Eilis he loves her after walking her home.
   Does this surprise you?

5. How does Eilis respond to Tony telling her that he loves her?
   What does this tell you about how she is feeling?

6. "Maybe, I feel the same way."
   Does Eilis love Tony, do you think?
   Why does she want to be with him?
   What makes this a significant moment in their relationship?

7. What does Eilis not want to talk about with Tony?
   Can you explain her outlook here?

8. "Oh Eilis, you know I'm by your side, even when I'm not."
   How is Rose feeling without her sister?

9. How does Tony react to seeing Eilis in her swimming costume?
Why does he respond this way?

10. Do Eilis and Tony have a serious relationship, in your view?
Give reasons for your opinion.

11. "Why did I ever come here?"
How does Eilis respond to the news of her sister's death?
How is she feeling?

12. Describe the phone conversation Eilis has with her mother.
What does it tell you about their relationship?

13. How does Tony feel about Eilis going home?
Does he understand how she feels?

14. "I don't need to think about it."
How does Eilis feel about Tony?
Do they have a strong relationship?

15. Why does Eilis turn up at Tony's in the middle of the night?

16. How does Tony respond when Eilis says she is going home to Ireland?
Does he trust her to come back, do you think?
Would you marry him, in her position?

17. What reason does Tony give Eilis for wanting to marry her?
    What do you consider his real reasons to be?

18. "Would a promise not be the same?"
    "If you can promise, you can easily do this."
    Does Eilis want to marry Tony, do you think?
    Is Tony being manipulative here?
    Explain what is going on here, as you see it.

19. Why do Eilis and Tony decide to have sex at this point?
    Why was the marriage proposal significant?

20. What does Tony and Eilis' decision to have sex tell us about their relationship?

21. After they have sex, Eilis asks Tony to stay with her. Comment on this and what it tells you about their relationship.

22. Does Eilis love Tony?

23. Does Tony love Eilis?

24. Does Tony support Eilis well during this time of grief?

25. What impact will Eilis' return to Ireland have on their relationship?

Part Three
Hero, Heroine, Villain

Eilis is settling in well to her new life. She is the first of Mrs Kehoe's girls to pass exams, showing that she is an exceptional character, bright, determined and hard-working.

She is happy now in New York, chatty and relaxed with Tony and his family.

When Tony tells Eilis that he loves her, she is unsure at first what to say. She is young and inexperienced, and this is all very new to her. She asks her housemate, Sheila, about marriage, trying to figure out if it is for her.

The next night, Eilis tells Tony that she feels the same way about him. She has found the words to tell Tony how she feels about him.

Eilis' innocence and inexperience is seen when she tells the other girls at Mrs Kehoe's about her trip to Coney Island. They are keen to prepare her, as is Miss Fortini, who fits her for a swimsuit. Eilis still has much to learn, but she accepts the guidance of these more experienced women in her life.

Eilis is enjoying life more, thanks to Tony, and her homesickness has passed.

Eilis is devastated by her sister's death. A sense of duty makes her want to go home, to her mother.

Tony asks Eilis to marry him before she leaves, and pushes the issue when she is reluctant. She does not want to rush into a marriage, as Tony does, but she bows to his wishes, and agrees.

They go to Eilis' room and consummate their relationship. This bold move shows that Eilis is prepared to take risks, and also, that she takes her relationship with Tony very seriously, feeling very strongly towards him.

Questions

1. How does Eilis impress Tony's parents?

2. How does Eilis respond when Tony tells her that he loves her?
   What does this tell you about Eilis?

3. What does Eilis ask Sheila about?
   What does this tell you about Eilis?

4. How does Eilis do in her exams?
   Are you surprised by this?
   Give reasons for your answer.

5. How does Eilis respond to the news of her sister's death?

6. "I don't need to think about it."
   How does Eilis feel about Tony?
   Is she committed to him, do you think?

7. What makes Eilis decide to go home?

8. Why, do you think, does Eilis agree to marry Tony?

Part Four

Summary

From 1.05.34 minutes (Eilis and Tony walking to City Hall) up to 1.27.29 minutes (Eilis finishes talking with the older woman).

- Eilis and Tony get married.

- Eilis returns home to her mother in County Wexford.

- Eilis goes out with Nancy and George, to find they have invited a young man, Jim Farrell, along too.

- Eilis tells her friends about living in Brooklyn. Jim encourages her to call in to Davis' for work, as they have not replaced Rose.

- Eilis goes to Davis' when they send for her, and is offered a part-time job.

- Eilis goes to the beach with Jim, George and Nancy.

- Tony asks his brother, Frankie, to help him write to Eilis.

- Eilis and Jim go out to eat together, and she goes to his home and meets his parents.

- Eilis and Jim sit together at George and Nancy's wedding. Afterwards, a local woman suggests it won't be long until Eilis and Jim are wed.

Part Four
Cultural Context/Social Setting

Eilis returns to Enniscorthy and sees her friend Nancy outside the church. Eilis' mother has promised Nancy that Eilis will go to her wedding, even though it means extending her stay. Eilis' mother feels it is fitting that Eilis should attend her best friend's wedding.

Eilis goes out with Nancy and George, and their friend Jim Farrell, who encourages her to go to Davis' for a job.

Home is comfortable and familiar for Eilis.

Eilis is offered a part-time job in Davis'. Enniscorthy has changed, and now has opportunities for her. Similarly, her developing relationship with Jim suggests that this is a place where she could be happy. Home is no longer empty of potential, but rather, holds a promising future.

Jim's family home is large and comfortable. He has wealth and a certain status in the town.

Nancy and George get married in church, with the whole community in attendance. Afterwards, an older woman suggests that it will not be long before Jim and Eilis marry. Eilis' friendship with Jim appears to others as a courtship. This is a public world, where lives and relationships are shared, and where there are clear expectations about settling down.

Questions

1. "A lot of you in Brooklyn."
   How are the Irish in Brooklyn portrayed in this text? Describe their lives in America, as you see them.

2. What is Eilis' mother doing with the letters of condolence she has received?
   What insight does this give you into this world?

3. How does Eilis feel about the men in the rugby club?
   What insight does this give you into Enniscorthy?

4. What does Jim say to Eilis about Rose's death?
   What insight does this give you into Eilis' community at home in Enniscorthy?

5. How does Eilis describe life in Brooklyn to Nancy?
   Is her description accurate? Why/why not?

6. What differences do you notice between Eilis' street and where she lives in Brooklyn?

7. "He'll be in that big house on his own."
   What is Eilis' mother telling her about Jim Farrell here?

8. What is the significance of Mr Brown offering Eilis part-time work?

9. "We don't really know anything of the rest of the world."
   Is Jim's comment about his community accurate, do you think?

10. The golf club is inaugurating a prize in Rose's name. What insight does this give you into this community?

11. Jim's mother wants to meet Eilis. Does this surprise you? What does this tell you about this world?

12. What are Jim's family and home like?

13. Are you surprised that local people may expect Jim and Eilis to marry? Give reasons for your answer. What does this tell you about this world? Is Enniscorthy very different from Brooklyn in this regard? Explain your point of view.

14. What does Nancy and George's wedding scene tell you about this world?

15. Does Eilis belong in the world of Enniscorthy? Give reasons in your answer, including examples to support your view.

Part Four
Literary Genre

Eilis and Tony are presented as a happy, hopeful couple, very much in love as they get married.

Once Eilis returns home, her mother is keen to keep her there, telling her to stay on for Nancy's wedding, and mentioning her own empty days. She is manipulating Eilis emotionally, using her sense of duty to make her feel guilty and stay in County Wexford. This potential source of conflict adds a slowly mounting tension to Eilis' stay.

Nancy invites Jim Farrell along on Eilis' first night out with her old friends as a potential love interest, knowing nothing of Eilis' marriage to Tony. Her connection with Jim Farrell and their developing relationship will further complicate Eilis' life at home, and the decision she will have to make about returning to Brooklyn.

Jim wants to see more of Eilis, and encourages her to go to Davis' to see about work. Her mother insists that she go and help out with their books, resulting in Eilis being offered a part-time job. Now it seems, Enniscorthy has a lot to offer Eilis, while Brooklyn is far off and removed.

Tony's letter is narrated to images of Eilis and Jim laughing and spending time together. There is tension and potential conflict here. Eilis is involved with two men, in two different countries, a situation that cannot be resolved without someone suffering unhappiness. As we hear Tony's words, and see Eilis and Jim sitting in his car laughing, this tension builds.

This tension is increased as Eilis does not read Tony's letter, but goes out to dinner with Jim and meets his family. She tries to write to Tony, but cannot find the words she needs. Clearly, Eilis is torn, undecided about what she should do.

Sitting in the church at Nancy and George's wedding, Jim glances at Eilis, imagining perhaps their future together, as she guiltily thinks of her husband who she has kept secret. Tension mounts as we realise this impossible situation cannot continue.

Questions

1. Comment on Eilis and Tony's wedding.
   Do they seem happy to you?
   What strikes you about the couple?

2. How is this wedding significant from a plot perspective?
   Explain how it impacts on the story.

3. "Do you wanna play?"
   Is Tony a likeable character?
   Give reasons for your answer.

4. Is Eilis happy or unhappy to be back in County Wexford?
   Is it hard for her to adjust to being home?
   Give reasons for your answer.

5. "You can wait an extra week to see your best friend married."
   What is Eilis' mother doing here?
   What does this indicate?

6. Describe the scene at Rose's grave.
   What does it reveal about what Eilis is thinking and how she is feeling?

7. How does Eilis react to seeing Jim in the car?
   What is Nancy doing here?

8. What are your first impressions of Jim?

9. "But you just want her to stay."
   Why does Jim tell Eilis to call in to Davis'?

10. Is Jim interested in Eilis, do you think?
    Is Eilis interested in Jim?
    Explain your view.

11. "He's a catch for someone."
    What is Eilis' mother doing here?

12. How does Jim make the storyline more exciting?

13. "Thank goodness you're back."
    Why is Eilis' mother so keen for her to go to Davis'?

14. How does the offer of a job at Davis' affect the storyline at this point?

15. What do you notice about the use of colour as Eilis and her friends climb the sand dune?
    How does music add to this scene?

16. How does Eilis respond to seeing the empty beach?
    What is the significance of this?

17. What does Eilis think of Jim?
    How does this impact on the story?

18. Eilis is the only one of her friends to have her swimsuit on under her clothes.
    What is being communicated to us here?

19. Why does Tony go to his brother, Frankie, for help?
    Comment on the timing of this scene.
    Why does it appear following the beach scene?

20. What is the effect of the voice-over of Tony's letter?
    Comment on the images that accompany it.
    What is being communicated to the audience?

21. Eilis does not read Tony's letter.
    What is being communicated to us here?
    What is your reaction to this?
    How does Eilis feel about Tony?
    Support your point of view.
    How does Eilis feel about Jim?
    Support your point of view.

22. What do you learn about Jim from his meal with Eilis?

23. How does Jim feel about Eilis?
    How do you know?
    How does the actor communicate this to us?

24. Why is Eilis struggling to write to Tony?

25. What does the church wedding scene add to the story?

26. Are we being made to feel that Eilis belongs in County Wexford?
    Explain your point of view.

27. How are Jim and Eilis' mother complicating matters for Eilis?
How does this affect the story?

28. What have you learned about Eilis in this section?

29. Has your view of Eilis' character changed after watching this section?
Give reasons for your answer.

30. Do you anticipate or expect a romantic relationship to develop between Jim and Eilis?
Why/why not?

31. What aspects of the story are becoming more exciting?
Be specific in your answer.

Part Four
General Vision and Viewpoint

Eilis speaks aloud at her sister's grave, wishing that things were different. The loss of her sister, who never got to experience New York or know Tony, is a cause of unhappiness for her.

Eilis' mother appears to be very lonely. From the moment Eilis arrives home, her mother tries to extend her stay, telling her to remain an extra week to go to Nancy's wedding. Eilis' mother endures her pain and suffering without saying a lot about it. She leads her sad, unhappy life, mostly alone.

Now that she is home, Enniscorthy has lots to offer Eilis, giving her many reasons to stay. Nancy is keen to set Eilis up with Jim Farrell, a match that Eilis' mother approves of. Rose's employer at Davis', Mr Brown, offers Eilis part-time work. It is perhaps a cruel coincidence that there are now so many reasons to remain in Ireland, when she left looking for a more fulfilling life. Eilis' predicament shows the complexity of life and how complicated and difficult life choices can be. Returning to Brooklyn will be hard, with so much to keep her at home.

Jim is a thoughtful, kind man with a clear interest in Eilis. She enjoys spending time with him, but it is difficult to feel good about Jim and Eilis, knowing that she is already married. In this way, the perspective is darkened by Eilis keeping Tony a secret. Whether she intends to or not, she is misleading Jim, as well as betraying Tony, and so is true to neither man.

This is, of course, a very difficult situation for Eilis to find herself in, and it is hard to know what the right thing for her to do is. In this way, we are offered an outlook that is not clear cut or easy to decipher. Eilis' difficult choice is messy and complicated, and someone is sure to be hurt. In this way, in the midst of a love story, the general vision and viewpoint is not entirely positive or optimistic, but is clouded by indecision, deceit by omission and future hurt feelings.

Questions

1. "Will we ever tell our children we did this?"
   How, do you think, does Eilis imagine her future life with Tony?
   Is she hopeful or hopeless?
   Explain your view.

2. "I wish everything was different."
   What do Eilis' words at her sister's grave reveal about how she is feeling?
   Is she happy with how things have turned out?
   Why/why not?

3. "It's not as if I've anything else to do."
   How is Eilis' mother feeling?
   Is her life full or empty, in your view?
   How does this make you feel?

4. Is Eilis' return home happy or sad?
   Give reasons for your answer.

5. Jim speaks to Eilis about Rose's death and funeral.
   What impact does this have on Eilis?
   What does it suggest about Jim and his outlook?

6. Both Nancy and Eilis' mother seem keen for Eilis to go out with Jim Farrell.
   How would this make you feel, if you were Eilis?
   What sort of situation has she found herself in?

7. Will deciding to go back to Brooklyn be an easy choice for Eilis to make?
   What is the director suggesting about life here?

8. "I wish it'd been like this before I went."
   What is troubling Eilis?
   What is she really wishing for here?
   How does this make you feel?
   What does this tell you about life?

9. Jim wants to travel.
   Comment on his outlook here.
   Is it positive or negative?
   How does his outlook add to the mood at this point?

Part Four
Relationships

Eilis and Nancy fit back into their roles of close friends. Nancy invites Jim Farrell out with them, thinking she is helping Eilis by introducing her to this attractive and available young man. Eilis has not told Nancy about Tony, her time away in New York has created some real distance between them that Nancy is unaware of.

Eilis and Jim get on well from the beginning, chatting comfortably, with Jim eager to know more about her. Their relationship develops as they spend more time together, with Eilis meeting his family.

There is an expectation that this relationship between Eilis and Jim will develop into something serious that is shared by Jim, his parents, Nancy, Eilis' mother, and perhaps even Eilis herself. They all make comments that suggest that this relationship becoming more serious would be very favourable indeed.

Coupled with this interest in Jim is Eilis' lack of communication with Tony. She does not read his letters, and cannot write one of her own. Her relationship with Tony is clearly jeopardised by her relationship with Jim.

This is very significant when considering the theme of relationships in this film. Is Eilis betraying Tony by allowing her friendship with Jim to develop? Is she being deceitful to Jim by keeping her marriage a secret? Both of these men are sincere and open in their affections towards Eilis, but she keeps something from both, showing how difficult and complicated even loving relationships can be.

Questions

1. Are you surprised that Eilis and Tony get married?
   Explain your view.
   Are they happy together?
   Give reasons for your answer.

2. Would you ever get married secretly like this?
   Why/why not?

3. Are Eilis and Nancy happy to see each other again?

4. "Your mother accepted the invitation on your behalf."
   What is Eilis' mother doing here?

5. How does Eilis describe Tony at her sister's grave?
   What insight does this give you into how she feels about him?

6. Why does Nancy invite Jim Farrell along when she meets Eilis?
   What does this tell you about Eilis' friendship with Nancy?

7. Do Eilis and Jim get on well?
   Use examples to support your view.

8. How do you feel about Eilis' developing relationship with Jim?
   Is she betraying Tony?
   Fully explain your point of view.

9. Eilis and Jim go out and eat together.
   Is this a date?
   What does it tell you about their relationship?

10. Eilis meets Jim's parents.
    How do you feel about this?
    How does he feel about her?
    Describe their relationship at this point, as you see it.

11. Eilis tries and fails to write to Tony.
    What, do you think, is she trying to say?
    Comment on their relationship, as you see it at this point.

12. How does Jim treat Mrs Lacey, Eilis' mother?
    How is this significant?

13. "Your mother will have a wonderful day out."
    Comment on the expectations of the woman who greets Eilis after the wedding mass.
    Is she jumping to conclusions or are her expectations fair?
    Give reasons for your answer.

14. Is Eilis attracted to Jim, in your opinion?
    Give reasons for your answer.

15. Do you expect Eilis to return to Tony or stay with Jim?
    Explain your point of view.

16. Which man do you want Eilis to choose?
    Give reasons for your answer.

Part Four
Hero, Heroine, Villain

Eilis settles back in to life at home, spending time with her mother, her friend Nancy, and visiting Rose's grave.

The others in her life want Eilis to stay in Enniscorthy. Nancy sets her up with Jim Farrell, a match her mother approves of, and both Jim and her mother encourage her to work at Davis'. Pressure is being put on Eilis to stay at home, as her family and friends know nothing of her commitment to Tony in Brooklyn.

Eilis goes along with their wishes to a certain extent. She says she is going back to New York, but does not push the issue, and mentions Tony to no-one. She is enjoying her time in Enniscorthy, and seems to be carried along by this rather than asserting herself.

Eilis spends a lot of time with Jim as their relationship develops. It is difficult to know whether Eilis still wants to go back to Tony. She goes out with Jim and meets his parents. Although she has not kissed Jim, in all other regards, she is filling the role of girlfriend, something she is aware of, as people keep commenting on it. However, she does not stop spending time with Jim. She is clearly torn between staying in Enniscorthy and returning to Tony and her future looks undecided.

Questions

1. Eilis and Tony are secretly married.
   Does Eilis love Tony, do you think?
   Is she happy to have married him?
   Give reasons for your answer.

2. "You all look the same. It's the blazer and the hair oil."
   How does Eilis treat Jim when she first meets him?
   Why, do you think, does she speak to him this way?

3. How does Mr Brown's offer of part-time work at Davis' make Eilis feel, do you think?
   Give reasons for your answer.

4. Is Eilis happy to be home?
   Give reasons for your answer.

5. Eilis is the only one of her friends to have her swimsuit on under her clothes.
   What does this tell you about her?

6. How do you feel about Eilis not reading Tony's letters or writing back to him?
   What insight does this give you into how she is feeling?
   What insight does it give you into her character?

7. Is Eilis interested in Jim, do you think?
   What makes you say this?

8. Is Eilis a deceitful character?
   Give reasons for your answer.

9. What has Eilis' return to County Wexford made you realise about her character?

Part Five

Summary

From 1.27.30 minutes (Eilis dances with Jim) to the end.

- Eilis and Jim dance together and he asks her to stay in Ireland.

- Mary comes to fetch Eilis for Miss Kelly. Miss Kelly reveals that she knows Eilis is married. Eilis stands her ground, asserting that she is married. As soon as she leaves, she books her passage to New York.

- Eilis tells her mother that she is married and is going home to New York. Her mother says goodbye and goes to bed, choosing not to talk about it.

- Jim reads a note from Eilis.

- Eilis gives a young girl advice on the boat to New York.

- Eilis is reunited with Tony.

Part Five
Cultural Context/Social Setting

Jim and Eilis' relationship has developed to the point where he is about to ask her to marry him. She still does not bring herself to mention Tony, knowing that to do so would shatter what is between them. However, in this world, the responsibility of marriage seems unavoidable, as she is about to be proposed to a second time. This formalising of emotional relationships is part of this world. It is not possible for Eilis to continue to drift along much longer without choosing between these men, as this world demands that she make this choice.

Miss Kelly's revelation of her knowledge of Eilis' marriage represents all that is spiteful, vicious and mean-spirited about Eilis' home community. The older woman relishes having this information as something to hold over Eilis.

Once Eilis calls herself Eilis Fiorello and asserts that she is a married woman, her return to Brooklyn is assured. She no longer wants to stay in a place like this, but also, the secrecy surrounding her marriage and her relationship with Jim Farrell would be much talked about.

Now that her marriage is no longer secret, Eilis cannot be involved with Jim as she was before. She has crossed a line in social etiquette by acting like a single woman when she was in fact a married one. Miss Kelly's delighted outrage is representative of that of the town.

In choosing New York, Eilis chooses Tony, and the future he has promised her. She is also rejecting the small world of Enniscorthy, where her private life may be the subject of gossip, for the freedom of starting afresh in America.

Questions

1. How has marriage impacted on Eilis, the decisions she makes, and her freedom?
   Explain your point of view fully, using examples to support your view.

2. How does Miss Kelly speak to Mary when Eilis comes to the shop?
   What gives Miss Kelly the right to speak to her this way? Why is her behaviour tolerated in this world, do you think?

3. "You know what people are like, they love to talk."
   What does Eilis' comment to Miss Kelly reveal about this community?
   Is her comment accurate, in your view?

4. "I'd forgotten what this town is like."
   What does Miss Kelly remind Eilis of?

5. Could Eilis stay in Enniscorthy and be with Jim now, in your view?
   Give reasons for your answer.

6. "People say there are so many Irish people there, it's like home."
   Is this an accurate representation of life in Brooklyn?
   Give reasons for your answer.

7. What is the appeal of New York for Eilis?
   What does this tell you about the world of the film?

Part Five
Literary Genre

Jim opens his heart to Eilis and asks her not to go back to America. This is an exciting moment, as it is difficult to know how Eilis will respond. Despite her marriage to Tony, she clearly feels a connection with Jim, and he is escalating matters by revealing how he feels about her. Pressure is mounting for Eilis, who seems carried along by her relationship with Jim, simultaneously a bystander and a participant. The pressure to make a decision and choose either Jim or Tony is building.

Miss Kelly sends for Eilis and viciously reveals that she knows of Eilis' wedding at City Hall. Eilis is not cowed by her old boss, but challenges her, asking her what she intended to do with such information. Eilis calls herself Eilis Fiorello and leaves. This is a tense, dramatic scene, as Miss Kelly attempts to manipulate and dominate Eilis with her discovery. In this moment of conflict, Eilis is assertive, owning her married title and standing up to Miss Kelly.

However, Eilis does not beat Miss Kelly on this occasion. Miss Kelly's knowledge sets in motion Eilis' return to America. The storm of gossip that will follow forces Eilis to act. In this way, the confrontation in this scene is exciting and dramatic, and also ends Eilis' indecision. In naming herself Eilis Fiorello, she has forsaken Jim, and the town of Enniscorthy, and committed to Tony and America.

Miss Kelly has brought about Eilis' decision in an exciting, dramatic way as she has the power to expose her secret marriage. Although it is satisfying to watch Eilis stand up to her old boss, it is somewhat unsatisfactory overall. Eilis has not made up her own mind, Miss Kelly has made it for her, robbing her of real choice.

Eilis' mother's reaction to the news that she is married, and leaving, adds sadness to the story. There is a gulf between these characters, they cannot communicate fully with one another or properly express how they feel. Eilis' mother goes to bed rather than speaking with her daughter, a sad situation that may suggest that Eilis' return to Brooklyn is the right decision. This emotional scene adds to the drama surrounding Eilis' departure.

Eilis sends Jim a note, telling him, one presumes, that she is leaving. This adds finality to her decision. However, she does not go to see Jim, we do not hear how she feels about him, nor do we see her upset over her decision. This absense of a conversation eases the transition to Eilis' departure. Also, we do not hear any reproachful words from Jim, and so, do not judge Eilis, or see her actions through his eyes.

Her conversation on deck with the young woman going to Brooklyn shows how much Eilis has grown and changed since she first went to New York, while simultaneously reminding us that she too is a young, hopeful girl, making her way in the world.

The story ends happily, with Eilis and Tony thrilled to be reunited and together again, and Eilis' life in Enniscorthy consigned to the past. She has chosen Tony and New York, and all that they represent.

Questions

1. Jim tells Eilis he does not want her to go back to America. Is this an exciting moment?
   How does it impact on the story?

2. What question is Jim saving for later?
   How does Eilis respond to Jim's declaration?

3. What, do you think, is Eilis thinking as she dances with Jim?
   How do you feel about the way Eilis is treating Tony and Jim?
   How does it affect your understanding of her character?

4. How does Miss Kelly speak to Mary when Eilis arrives at the shop?

5. "You can't fool me, Miss Lacey."
   Why has Miss Kelly sent for Eilis?
   Why is this a significant development?

6. How does Eilis react to Miss Kelly's revelation?
   What does this show you about Eilis' character?

7. Is this confrontation a tense and exciting moment in the story?
   Give reasons for your answer.

8. Why does Eilis book her ticket immediately after her exchange with Miss Kelly?
   What does this add to the story?

9. Is the story moving very rapidly at this point?
   Is this effective pacing?
   Explain your view.

10. Describe the scene at dinner as Eilis tells her mother she is leaving.
    Is this an emotional scene?
    What impact does it have on the audience?
    Give reasons for your answer.

11. What is the atmosphere like as Eilis prepares to leave Ireland?

12. Eilis leaves Jim a note.
    What, do you think, does it say?
    Why has the director not included a voice-over of the note, do you think?

13. How important is music in helping to build atmosphere in this closing section?

14. What is the effect of Eilis' conversation with the young woman on deck?
    What does it add to the story?
    Is Eilis similar to this young woman? Why/why not?

15. What is the effect of hearing Eilis' advice to this girl?

16. Comment on the film's final moments, where Tony is reunited with Eilis.
    How does this make you feel?
    Is this a happy ending?

17. Is this a good ending?
    Is this a satisfying ending?
    Give reasons to support your point of view.

Part Five
General Vision and Viewpoint

It is difficult not to feel sorry for Jim, and indeed, Eilis, as he reveals how he feels about her and asks her not to return to America. Jim cares about Eilis, and she cares about him, and were it not for her hasty marriage to Tony, there would be nothing stopping them from being together. However, the fact that Eilis has kept her marriage to Tony a secret from Jim is problematic. She has not been honest with Jim, or her husband. Indeed, it is hard to know if Eilis has been honest with herself, as she does not choose one man over the other, but has allowed the situation to escalate.

The outlook here suggests that life is complex and unpredictable, and shows that life choices are difficult, and also perhaps, that it is impossible not to hurt others as we follow our own hearts. Eilis' indecision and secretive relationships are unfair to these men. She has found herself in a situation where she must hurt someone, whether she intends to or not. By pretending too long that she does not have to choose, Eilis has misled Jim and made him believe that he has a future with her.

Miss Kelly sends for Eilis to darkly reveal that she knows of her marriage. She does this to yield power over Eilis, her motives are mean-spirited, unkind and manipulative.

However, Eilis bravely stands up to Miss Kelly, confirming her married status, robbing Miss Kelly of whatever power she wanted to hold over her.

Although Eilis standing up to Miss Kelly is a brave, positive moment, it is underscored by negativity, as Eilis is pushed and forced into acknowledging Tony instead of doing so out of love.

Eilis may appear as the victor in the exchange with Miss Kelly, but in besting the older woman, she commits to returning to America and losing Jim. Miss Kelly has robbed her of her choice, and perhaps of her dream of a life in Enniscorthy. The older woman has forced her hand, and Eilis has no option but to choose Tony this way.

It is a little sad that it took circumstances like these for Eilis to acknowledge Tony, the man she has married and is supposed to love.

It is also sad when Eilis tells her mother that she is married and is going back to America, and her mother says goodbye and goes to bed. This mother-daughter relationship is deeply flawed. Eilis and her mother care about each other, but cannot talk or communicate properly, something very sad that darkens the film's outlook.

Eilis sends Jim a note, but does not go to see him before she leaves. It is an abrupt ending for him, but Eilis does not dwell on this, looking forward instead to her return to New York.

The film ends on a happy, hopeful note, with Eilis and Tony delighted to be reunited. Eilis has made her decision and the storyline has been resolved, ending on a positive note.

Questions

1. What does Jim want to talk about with Eilis?
   Why does he want to talk about this?
   How does this make you feel?
   Is Eilis being fair to Jim, in your view?
   How does this make you feel?

2. Was it selfish of Eilis to have kept Tony a secret from everyone at home?
   What does Eilis' secrecy suggest about human nature?
   Give reasons for your answer.

3. "The world is a small place, isn't it?"
   Why has Miss Kelly sent for Eilis?
   What is Miss Kelly's motivation?
   What, exactly, is Miss Kelly trying to achieve?
   What does this tell you about human nature?

4. Eilis accuses Miss Kelly of not knowing what she would do, after revealing that Eilis is married.
   Do you think this is the case?
   Why then, did she send for Eilis?

5. Eilis stands up to Miss Kelly, calling herself Eilis Fiorello.
   Is this a triumphant moment? Why/why not?
   What is the atmosphere like at his point in the story?

6. Eilis cries as she tells her mother that she is married.
   Why has she decided to tell her mother the truth?

What does the secrecy surrounding Eilis' marriage add to the general vision and viewpoint?

7. Did Eilis want to be secretly married before she came home?
   Do you feel sorry for her here?

8. What is the author suggesting about secrecy and deception and how it impacts on people's lives?

9. Eilis tells her mother that she wants to be with Tony.
   Do you believe her?

10. Why, do you think, does she reveal her commitment to Tony now?
    How does this make you feel?
    Is Eilis' pledge to Tony motivated by positive or negative reasons?
    Explain your point of view.

11. How does Eilis' mother respond to the news that Eilis is married and leaving in the morning?
    How does this make you feel?
    Have Eilis and her mother let each other down?
    Explain your point of view.

12. Do regret and disappointment affect the general vision and viewpoint here?
    Use examples to support your view.

13. How do you feel about Eilis' decision to return to Brooklyn?

>   Is she making the right choice, in your view?
>   Give reasons for your answer.
>
> 14. Eilis leaves a note for Jim, telling him of her departure, but does not go to see him.
>   How does this make you feel?
>   Is Eilis being selfish here, or is she protecting herself emotionally?
>
> 15. Does Eilis' return to Brooklyn, and Tony, feel like a positive or negative development to you?
>   Give reasons for your answer.
>
> 16. Is Eilis kind to the girl on deck?
>   What does this tell you about people and human nature?
>
> 17. "This is where your life is."
>   Is this a happy ending?
>   Fully explain your point of view.
>
> 18. Does Eilis' time with Jim in Ireland matter?
>   Does her time with Jim affect her love for Tony?
>   Explain your view.
>
> 19. What is the director telling us about love and life in this film?
>   How does this make you feel?
>
> 20. How does Eilis feel about Tony as the film ends?
>   How does this affect the general vision and viewpoint?

21. Will Eilis and Tony be happy, do you think?
    Explain your point of view.

22. Will Eilis' mother and Jim be happy?
    Does their happiness impact on the general vision and viewpoint?
    Explain your point of view.
    How does the future happiness of characters impact on the general vision and viewpoint as the story ends?
    Explain your point of view.

23. Has Eilis grown and matured over the course of the film?
    Has she discovered her own identity and path in life by the end of the film?
    Does this have a positive or negative effect on the film's outlook?
    Give reasons for your answer.

24. How do you feel as the film ends?
    What makes you feel this way?

Part Five
Relationships

Jim asks Eilis to stay in Ireland as he is about to propose to her. Eilis does not tell him about Tony, or tell him that their relationship cannot develop further. Clearly, Eilis cares about Jim, and whether or not she believes a life with him may be possible, she cannot bring herself to tell him that she is not available. Perhaps she is considering staying in Ireland with Jim, and so keeps her marriage a secret.

However, although Jim's feelings for Eilis are very warm and positive, her secrecy here has a negative impact on this relationship. Eilis cares about Jim, but does not reveal the truth to him, which is selfish and so impacts negatively on the theme of relationships.

Miss Kelly sends for Eilis to manipulate and dominate her by revealing her knowledge of Eilis' marriage in New York. Eilis stands up to her old boss, acknowledging her marriage, and in so doing, ensures her return to Tony, and the loss of Jim.

Although Eilis announces that she is indeed married here, the circumstances are not a great way for her to break the news of having a husband. The way that she is forced to admit to her marriage also impacts negatively on the theme of relationships; Eilis is not happily telling everyone about her husband, but rather admits to her secret when she is backed into a corner.

Later, Eilis tells her mother that she wants to be with her husband. She reaffirms her commitment to Tony in revealing that she is married. Now that Miss Kelly has forced her to admit to being a married woman, she commits to Tony, and wants to go to him immediately.

Eilis' mother asks very little about him, saying goodnight and going to bed. Although she and Eilis care about each other, they are incapable of communicating properly, or really sharing a close bond. This relationship is lacking, causing each of them sadness. Eilis's tear-filled conversation with her mother shows the negative, flawed relationships in the film.

Jim receives a note from Eilis, telling him of her departure, but she does not go to see him. Perhaps this is because she cannot face him, perhaps she simply chooses not to, now that her heart is set on returning to Tony.

In her voice-over in the closing moments, Eilis refers to someone who has no connection to the past, someone who is yours alone. For Eilis, this special someone is Tony. She is joyfully reunited with him, happy to have come back to him. The final image of Eilis and Tony together is very positive. They are presented as a young couple, very much in love.

Questions

1. What does Jim want to talk to Eilis about?
   What does this tell you about how he feels about her?

2. "Your life here could be just as good. Better, even, maybe."
   Why, do you think, is Eilis torn between these men?

3. Eilis holds Jim close as they dance.
   Is she betraying Tony, in your view?
   Give reasons for your answer.

4. Does Eilis love Jim, in your opinion?
   Give reasons for your answer.

5. Why does Miss Kelly send for Eilis?

6. What impact does Eilis' confrontation with Miss Kelly have on her other relationships?

7. Why, do you think, does Eilis cry as she tells her mother that she is married?
   How would you feel if you were her mother?
   How does her mother react?

8. Eilis says that she wants to be with Tony.
   Do you think this is really the case?
   What has helped Eilis to reach this realisation?

9. Has Eilis been staying in Ireland for her mother's sake?
   Explain your point of view.

10. "I'd like to say goodbye now."
    How does Eilis' mother react to the news that she is leaving?
    What does this tell you about their relationship?

11. Does Eilis' mother love her, do you think?
    Can you explain why she chooses not to see Eilis again before her departure?

12. Does Eilis love her mother?
    Can you explain why their relationship is so fraught?

13. Eilis sends Jim a note before she leaves, but does not go to see him.
    What does this tell you about how Eilis feels about Jim?
    Is she treating him fairly here?

14. Does Jim love Eilis, in your opinion?
    Is this a positive or negative portrayal of a relationship?
    Give reasons for your answer.

15. Will Eilis tell Tony about Jim, do you think?
    Give reasons for your answer.

16. Was Tony right to doubt Eilis' return?
    What insight does this give you into their relationship?

17. "Someone who's only yours."
    How does Eilis feel about Tony, as the story ends?
    Explain why she feels this way about him.

18. How does Tony feel about Eilis as the film ends?
    How has their relationship changed over the course of the film?
    Do they have a good relationship?
    Give reasons for your answer.

Part Five
Hero, Heroine, Villain

Eilis allows Jim to think that they have a future together, not setting him straight when he asks her to stay in Ireland, and makes his intention to propose to her very clear. She seems to care a lot about him, and may want to believe that this future that he speaks of is possible. However, by not telling him the truth, she acts selfishly, knowing that his feelings will be hurt in the long run, but keeping the truth of her marriage from him anyway.

Eilis stands up to Miss Kelly when Miss Kelly tries to use her knowledge of Eilis' marriage against her. She does not allow Miss Kelly to control her or speak down to her. However, her impulsive decision to call herself Eilis Fiorello means that she must return to America. Perhaps she needed this outburst to make clear to her what she wants in life. Eilis is torn between her desire to return to Brooklyn, and wanting to stay in Enniscorthy, but Miss Kelly cruelly takes this decision from her. Miss Kelly reminds her of all the negatives of Enniscorthy, and Eilis rejects this place in favour of Tony, and New York.

The fact that Eilis has kept her marriage a secret from her mother saddens her, and she cries as she tells her mother this news.

Eilis does not go to see Jim, sending him a note instead. Whether this is to spare her feelings and not have to explain everything in person is unclear, perhaps she simply wants to leave as quickly as possible.

Her conversation with the young woman on deck shows how much Eilis has grown and learned in a short time, while also reminding us of her own vulnerability and youth as she is not so different to the girl she gives advice to.

Eilis has had to make many tough decisions over the course of the film. As the film ends, she is happy to be back with Tony, confident in her choice to return to someone who is just hers.

Questions

1. Jim asks Eilis not to return to America.
   Why doesn't Eilis tell him that she is married?
   Has Eilis betrayed Tony by allowing her relationship with Jim to develop to this point?
   Has Eilis purposely misled Jim by keeping Tony a secret?

2. What do you learn about Eilis from the way she treats Jim?
   Use examples to support your ideas.

3. Does the way Eilis treats Tony and Jim affect how you view her character?
   Be specific in your answer.

4. Why is Eilis so upset when she tells her mother that she is married?

5. What stops Eilis from following her mother upstairs to talk to her, in your view?
   How must this make Eilis feel?

6. Is Eilis selfish in the way she treats Jim and Tony?
   Give reasons for your answer.

7. What does Eilis' conversation with the young woman on the boat, and the advice she gives her, tell you about Eilis?

8. Is Eilis happy to be back with Tony as the film ends?
   How do you know?

9. Does Eilis feel that she belongs in New York? Give reasons for your answer.

10. Is Eilis a typical young woman? Fully explain your point of view, using examples to support your ideas.

11. Is Eilis a likeable character? Give reasons for your answer.

12. Is Eilis a relatable character? Give reasons for your answer.

The Comparative Study

Cultural Context/Social Setting

Cultural Context/Social Setting refers to the world of the text. Consider social norms, beliefs, values and attitudes.

Brooklyn takes place in 1950s Enniscorthy and New York, and the timeframe adds a lot to the setting.

Eilis' move to America is very significant due to the distance she is travelling. This is apparent when Rose dies and she cannot make it home for her funeral, but has to settle for her mother's description of the event on the telephone. Even this call itself reflects the cultural context, as Eilis has to wait in Father Flood's office for the call to come through; she is remote and distanced from home because of the limitations of travel and communications of the 1950s.

The town of Enniscorthy, as the film begins, is itself much of the reason why Eilis is emigrating, as she cannot get work and does not have a boyfriend. New York will offer her possibilities and potential, as a job has been arranged for her by Father Flood, a connection of her sister's.

In New York, Eilis is very much a part of the Irish population, living with other Irish girls and going to a weekly Irish dance. The Christmas Day lunch Father Flood arranges shows how difficult life away from home can be, as these forgotten Irish men have nothing in their lives, but cannot return home.

Father Flood's presence in the story shows how central the Church was to the lives of Irish people during this time. He has standing and influence in his community; he arranges Eilis' job, and is respected by Bartocci's store manager, who sends for him when Eilis suffers from homesickness.

It is also the night classes that he arranges for Eilis that show that through hard work and application, opportunites are available in New York. When Eilis returns to Enniscorthy, she is offered part-time work in Davis' because of the night classses she has completed. Her study in America unlocks work options for her back at home that were not previously available to her.

In both Enniscorthy and New York, female characters are pre-occupied with securing husbands for themselves. Nancy wants to go out with George Sheridan in Enniscorthy, the girls of Mrs Kehoe's attend dances in the hope of meeting a man. Indeed, once Eilis begins to date Tony, the other girls in Mrs Kehoe's are much warmer towards her, as now they have a shared interest and something to talk about. This focus on men is also seen when Eilis returns to Enniscorthy and her friend Nancy immediately tries to set her up with Jim Farrell, a match that Eilis' mother approves of due to Jim's wealth.

With such a focus on finding a man, it is not surprising that marriage is so central and significant to these characters' lives. Tony pushes for a secret marriage before Eilis leaves, knowing that such a serious commitment is not one she will take lightly. It is this secret bond to Tony that hinders her from becoming fully involved with Jim. As their society dictates, Jim also proposes marriage once they have grown close, putting Eilis in a complicated and difficult position.

Miss Kelly's confrontation with Eilis underlines how significant marriage is in this world. She uses her knowledge of Eilis' marriage as something to hold over her, as she is aware of the relationship between Eilis and Jim. Once Miss Kelly makes this known to her, Eilis has little option but to return to America. In this moment, Miss Kelly demonstrates the gossiping, interfering nature of the people of Enniscorthy. She delights in revealing what she knows about Eilis as sensational and scandalous. Miss Kelly shows that Enniscorthy is a place of judgement and gossip, where people are interested in other people's business.

In comparison, America offers freedom and potential, as everyone and everything is new, and this is shown in Eilis' relationship with Tony, a young Italian man she would not have met at home.

1. Briefly describe the world of County Wexford in this film.
   Briefly describe the world of New York in this film.
   Are the two worlds very different?
   Explain your point of view.
   What similarities do they share?

2. Does Eilis experience a broad range of people and culture in New York?
   Why/why not?
   What does this tell you about Eilis' world?
   Explain your point of view.

3. What is the role of women in the world of the film?
   What expectations are there for women in this world?
   Are women treated very differently in Enniscorthy and New York?
   Use examples to support your ideas.

4. Is Brooklyn a fun place for Eilis to live?
Are there opportunities for her at home?
Explain your point of view.

5. Is the world of Brooklyn a difficult place for Eilis to negotiate?
Give reasons for your answer.

6. Eilis chooses New York over Enniscorthy in this film.
What makes her choose New York?
Focus on the world of New York and the world of Enniscorthy in your answer.
Are you surprised that Eilis chooses to return to Tony, and the world of New York?

7. If the cultural context/social setting were different, would Eilis' relationships with Tony and Jim have been easier?
Use examples to support the points that you make.

8. Bearing the cultural context/social setting in mind, does Eilis act like Jim's girlfriend?
Does she act like his girlfriend by today's standards?
Explain your point of view.

9. How does Eilis' time in New York change her view of Enniscorthy?
Use examples to support your view.

10. Is the world of *Brooklyn* very traditional and rigid?
Give reasons for your answer.

11. Does the world of *Brooklyn* make it easy or difficult for characters to be happy?
Use examples to support your ideas.

12. Is marriage significant in this world?
Use examples to support your point of view.

13. What does the setting of the film tell you about the world of the characters?
Be specific in your answer.

14. What does this film suggest about adulthood and maturity?
Give reasons for your answer.

15. What is the role of women in the world of this film?

16. What is the role of men in the world of this film?

17. Are money, wealth and property important in this world?

18. Is school and academia important in this world?

19. What is valued in the world of this film?
What does this tell you about this place?

Literary Genre

Literary Genre refers to the way the story is told. Consider aspects of narration such as the manner and style of narration, characterisation, setting, tension, literary techniques, etc.

Character

Eilis grows and develops as a character over the course of the film. She is uncertain of herself and inexperienced in the world as she sets sail for America, but she grows in confidence and independence during the story, finally making life choices for herself and choosing the man she wants to be with. Her vulnerability makes her very likeable and relatable.

It is significant that both Tony and Jim are presented as kind, loving men, with a lot to offer Eilis. The fact that they are both good characters complicates her choice, as either one could make her happy. In this way, their characters themselves add to the love story dilemma.

Soundtrack

The soundtrack helps to set the tone through much of the film, adding to the visual imagery to build drama and emotion.

Tension

Most of the film's tension revolves around Eilis' choice between staying in Ireland with Jim or returning to Tony in America. The fact that her marriage to Tony is a secret adds to the tension as her mother and friends encourage her to pursue Jim, while she guiltily thinks of her husband. This decision adds uncertainty to the storyline and is very emotionally involving for the viewer, as we wonder what Eilis will do.

Conflict

There is conflict in the scene where Miss Kelly spitefully reveals that she knows of Eilis' marriage. She is accusatory and malicious in the way she speaks to Eilis here, but Eilis defiantly acknowledges her married state, and refuses to be cowed by her old employer. This confrontation, while exciting in itself, is very significant from a plot perspective, as it forces Eilis to reach a decision about Tony and Jim. Once Miss Kelly mentions that she knows Eilis is married, Eilis has little option other than returning to Tony, as we assume that word of her Italian husband will spread through the town.

Symbolism

The world of Brooklyn and New York represents possibility and potential. Far from home, Eilis makes a new life for herself, with a new job, qualifications and an Italian husband. In this way, Tony represents this world of opportunity, while Jim represents a life at home in Enniscorthy. These men are more than characters, they symbolise the paths in life that Eilis must choose.

1. How is this story told? (Consider the film format).
   Why is the story told in this way?
   What is the effect of this?

2. How does the film's opening arouse your interest and curiosity?

3. What are your first impressions of Eilis?
   Does your view of her change during the film?
   Explain your point of view.

4. Where does this story take place?
   Be specific in your answer.

5. How important is the love story between Eilis and Tony in this film?

6. How significant a plot point is Rose's death?
   Explain your point of view.

7. Does Tony represent (symbolise) Eilis' future in this film, do you think?
   Give reasons for your answer.

8. In what ways are the characters of Tony and Jim similar?
   How are they different?
   What does this add to the story?

9. How has Enniscorthy changed when Eilis returns following Rose's death?
   How does this affect the storyline?

10. Is Jim a superficial character?
    Is he simply a plot device to introduce conflict?
    Explain your point of view.

11. Are Jim's feelings and the hurt he experiences undeveloped in the film?
    Why is this the case?

12. Is Eilis a coward, who runs away from her problems?
    Give reasons for your answer.

13. Is Saoirse Ronan well-cast as Eilis?
    What does she bring to this role?
    Would another actress be as convincing, in your opinion?
    Give reasons for your answer.

14. Is this a simple or complex story?
    Explain your point of view.

15. Who would enjoy this story?
    Who is this story intended for?
    Give reasons for your answer.

16. What makes us invest ourselves emotionally in Eilis' choice in this film?

17. Is Eilis' character likeable?
    Give reasons for your answer.
    Is Eilis' character relatable?
    Give reasons for your answer.
    How does Eilis' character grow and develop over the course of the film?
    Give reasons for your answer.

18. Eilis is a young, inexperienced young woman, who goes to live in a new country.
    How does her character add to the storytelling in this film?

19. What obstacles is Eilis met with over the course of the film?
    How well does she deal with these difficulties?
    Include examples in your answer.

20. Is Eilis a good lead character?
    Explain your point of view.

21. Would you go on holidays with Eilis? Why/why not?
    Would you trust Eilis with your car/phone/house keys? Why/why not?

22. Is there humour in this film?
    How does it add to the story?

23. Does this film have a happy ending?
    What makes it happy/unhappy?
    Be specific in your answer.
    Is it a satisfying ending?
    Explain your point of view.

24. Do you think the cast for this film were well chosen?
    Explain your point of view.
    How do the actors enhance and add to the way the story is told?

25. What music is used in the soundtrack?
    How does the soundtrack add to the storytelling?

26. How does seeing and hearing the characters add to the storytelling?

27. Is this a very visual text?
    How does it compare with your other texts in this regard?
    How does this impact on your enjoyment of the story?

28. Comment on the mood as the story ends.

29. How does setting contribute to the story?
    Do you find this film to be interesting and easy to follow?

30. What draws the audience into this story?
    Highlight specific aspects of the text in your answer.

31. Where does the director create a bright, sunny mood to the story?
    How do they achieve this?

32. Where does the director create a sad, unhappy mood to the story?
    How do they achieve this?

33. Where do you see conflict in this story?
    How does the use of conflict add to this story?

34. Is this a realistic story?
    Support your view.

35. Is this story predictable?
    Did you expect Eilis to make the choice she does?

36. Did you enjoy this story?
    Use examples from the text to support your answer.

37. Who is your favourite character in this film?
    What makes you like/admire them?

38. Who is your least favourite character in this film?
    What makes you dislike them?

39. What themes can you identify in this story?

40. Is this film about choices?
Explain your view.

41. Is this film about self-discovery?
Explain your view.

42. In an interview, Saoirse Ronan (who plays Eilis) said "the film is basically about a choice that's being made…it's her being grown-up enough and mature enough, and experienced enough to make that choice."
Do you agree that Eilis' choice is central to the story?
Give reasons for your answer.
Do you agree that Eilis' character and her ability to make the right choice is central to the story?
Give reasons for your answer.

General Vision and Viewpoint

General Vision and Viewpoint refers to the author's outlook or view of life and how this viewpoint is represented in the text.

Brooklyn offers a mixed general vision and viewpoint. There are many bright, positive aspects to the film; Eilis' sister makes huge sacrifices out of love, to make sure her sister has a better life, Eilis' life in New York is full of possibility and potential, and the love stories with Tony and Jim suggest a life full of love and warmth.

Also, Eilis grows and matures over the course of the film. This self-discovery through travel and experience is a positive aspect worth noting.

However, there are also more negative aspects of the general vision and viewpoint to consider. Rose suffers alone, revealing her illness to no-one, suggesting a very lonely life and death. Eilis' mother is a very isolated figure, who cannot even bring herself to speak openly with her only daughter, which also paints a very sad, bleak, lonely picture of life.

Also, Eilis' affair with Jim, while married to Tony, shows not just how complex, but how cruel love can be. Tony never knows that Eilis dances with another, or meets the parents of another man who think their son is about to propose marriage. Similarly, Jim does not know that Eilis is married as they begin to see each other. Eilis somehow finds herself betraying and mistreating those who love her, which has a negative impact on the view of life the film captures. She never sets out or intends to hurt either Jim or

Tony, but not writing to Tony, and sending Jim a note at the end to explain her departure, are selfish acts.

The writer offers a view of life that is realistic, difficult and trying, while simultaneously being full of love and potential. The impact of Eilis' secrets and the difficult relationships she has with her mother and Miss Kelly, added to her sister's secret illness, prevent the outlook from being overwhelmingly positive. Instead, a more mixed general vision and viewpoint is offered.

1. Are there opportunities for Eilis in County Wexford as the film begins?
   Why does she go to America?
   Is this an easy decision for her?

2. Is it difficult for Eilis to settle in to life in New York?
   What does this suggest about life?

3. What does Rose's sudden death reveal to you about life?

4. What is it like for Eilis when she returns home after her sister's death?
   Does she have opportunities at home now?
   What does this tell you about life?
   How does this make you feel?

5. Eilis does not read Tony's letters.
   Is this a cold gesture?
   How does this make you feel?

6. What stops Eilis from telling her mother and friends about Tony?
   How does this make you feel?

7. Why does Eilis choose to return to Tony?
   Are Eilis' reasons positive or negative, in your view?
   How does this affect the general vision and viewpoint of the film?

8. Is this a film about a girl torn between two men, or a film about a girl who calculates what each man can offer her?
   How does your view of Eilis' actions impact on the film's general vision and viewpoint?

9. Rose sacrifices a lot for Eilis.
   What does this tell you about people, and life?
   Does it show the positive or negative side of human nature?

10. Do regret or loneliness affect the general vision and viewpoint of this film?
    Give reasons for your answer.

11. Does Eilis abandon her mother at the end of the film?
    Is she cruel to turn her back on Jim like this?
    How do her actions here affect the mood of the ending?

12. Does Eilis truly love Tony, in your view?
    How does this affect the film's general vision and viewpoint?

13. What do Eilis' relationships with Tony and Jim suggest about love?
    Is this a warm or cold view of human relationships?

14. Does this film offer a cold, or complicated view of love?
    Give reasons for your answer.
    How does this affect the view of life offered in the film?

15. Do characters in this film have opportunities and the potential for happiness?
    How does this add to the film's outlook?
    What does it suggest about life?

16. What do Eilis' experiences show you about people and life?

17. As the film ends, do you feel optimistic about Eilis and Tony's future?
    Give a reason for your answer.
    Are you happy with how things have turned out?

18. Does Eilis have an optimistic, hopeful approach to life?
    Do the other characters share this approach to life?
    What does this behaviour suggest about life?

19. Is love sure to succeed in this world?
    Explain your point of view.

20. Are characters in this text hopeful and forward looking about life?
    Are they realistic? Do they make well-thought out plans?
    What does this suggest about their outlook in life?

21. What does this film suggest about human nature?
    Is this outlook positive or negative?

22. Is there a lesson or moral to this story?
What could it be?

23. Does the film end on a hopeful or hopeless note?

24. Is life to be enjoyed or endured in the world of this text?
Refer to the film to support your ideas.

25. What is the message behind this film?
What is the director, John Crowley, telling us about life in this story?
Is this an encouraging, uplifting or depressing outlook?
Give reasons for your answer.

Theme/Issue
Relationships

Relationships has been selected as the theme/issue to explore in relation to this text.

The theme of relationships can be applied to any relationship in a text and includes love, marriage, friendship and family bonds. Consider the complexities of relationships and the impact they have on characters' lives.

The relationships in *Brooklyn* are one of the most compelling aspects of the story. Eilis finds herself involved emotionally with two men, in two different countries, who know nothing of each other.

Her relationship with Tony is very romantic and loving. He thinks very highly of her, meeting her after night class and telling her he loves her. Tony's youth and enthusiasm add to the romance of this relationship, he is a devoted boyfriend, eager to spend time with Eilis. Eilis reciprocates Tony's feelings, and it is him that she turns to after her sister's death. The only negative note comes when Eilis says she is going home to Ireland and Tony pushes for them to secretly marry. Eilis is not convinced that this is what she wants, asking him if a promise would not be the same thing, but Tony insists that they are wed. His insistence here, borne of love and attachment to Eilis, suggests a certain insecurity and fear that she will not return.

Perhaps his fears are justified, as once home in Enniscorthy, Eilis finds herself in a relationship with Jim. Jim also admires Eilis and wants to spend time with her, and he too proposes to her. Eilis cares about Jim and cannot bring herself to tell him about Tony, and so misleads Jim while betraying her husband. This shows the complexity and difficulty of relationships; Eilis cares about both of these men, but in doing so, she hurts them both.

Her love affairs are complicated and difficult, she struggles with maintaining her distance from Jim when she is attracted to him, and Tony is so far away. In this way, Eilis' relationships are portrayed as being very human and difficult, but also very intense and loving.

Eilis leaves and returns to New York without saying goodbye to Jim, ending their time together with a note, an abrupt and perhaps unfair way to end things.

Other relationships in the text have difficulties. Eilis and Rose care enormously for one another, yet Rose keeps her illness a secret from her. Eilis and her mother also care about each other, but are incapable of communicating openly and honestly with each other, and so Eilis leaves without having a proper conversation about Tony with the only family she has left.

There is a certain balance in Eilis' destructive relationship with Miss Kelly and the nurturing relationship she has with Father Flood. In this text, characters experience both positive, loving relationships, and difficult destructive ones, just as in real life. The complexities and emotion of human relationships are explored through Eilis' interactions, friendships and love affairs. Overall, relationships are positive and full of the potential for love and feeling, while the negative, destructive powers of spite and poor communication are also to be seen.

1. Could you leave your family, as Eilis does when she emigrates to New York?

2. Do Eilis and Tony have a very romantic relationship? Give reasons for your answer.

3. What strengths do you see in Eilis and Tony's relationship?

4. What weaknesses or problems do you see in Eilis and Tony's relationship?

5. What complicates Eilis and Tony's relationship?

6. Are Eilis and Tony a good match?
   Explain your view.

7. How does Eilis and Tony's relationship change and develop over the course of the story?
   Is this a positive or negative relationship?

8. Is Tony manipulative and controlling or romantic and spontaneous when he encourages Eilis to marry him?
   Is he fair to her here?
   Give reasons for your answer.

9. Does Eilis betray Tony?
   Explain your point of view.

10. Do Eilis and Jim have a good relationship?
    Explain your view.

11. Is Eilis' relationship with Jim the result of being nostalgic about being home?
    Is it Jim, or being home in Enniscorthy that fuels this relationship?
    Give reasons for your answer.

12. Is Eilis only ever friends with Jim?
    Give reasons for your answer.

13. Was Eilis just friends with Tony to begin with, or was it always romantic?

14. How is Eilis' relationship with Jim different to the early days of her relationship with Tony?
    How are they the same?
    Does Eilis betray Tony, and if so, on what grounds?

15. Does Eilis pretend to be single to Jim?

16. Would Eilis have returned to Tony, if she had not been caught out by Miss Kelly, in your opinion?
    Explain your point of view.

17. Does Eilis treat Tony and Jim badly?
    Give reasons for your answer.

18. Does Eilis' relationship with Jim impact on her relationship with Tony?
    Will she tell him about Jim, do you think?

19. In an interview, Saoirse Ronan (who plays the part of Eilis) said "the beautiful and heartbreaking thing...about

the two guys in it is that they're both wonderful and they both offer her security in different ways."
To what extent do you agree with this statement?
Refer to the film to support the points you make.

20. Is Eilis' relationship with Miss Kelly one of the most significant in the story?
Give reasons for your answer.

21. Is Eilis a good friend to Nancy?
Explain your view.

22. Eilis and her mother have a very open and honest conversation on the phone after Rose's death.
What does their conversation at this time reveal about their relationship?
What stops them from being so open and honest with each other again?

23. Does Eilis have a good relationship with her mother?
Does her mother love and support her?
What flaws do you see in their relationship?
Use examples to support your ideas.

24. Does Eilis have a good relationship with her sister, Rose?
Is Rose devoted to Eilis?
Does Eilis feel the same way about her sister?
Is this a positive portrayal of relationships?
Explain your point of view.
Would Eilis have stayed in Enniscorthy after returning home if Rose were still alive, do you think?

25. Are relationships in this text very complicated?
    Explain your point of view.

26. What stops characters from loving freely and saying exactly how they feel?
    Use examples to support your ideas.

27. Overall, are relationships depicted positively or negatively in this text?
    Use examples to support your point of view.

Hero, Heroine, Villain

'Hero, Heroine, Villain' refers to studying central characters (protagonists/antagonists).

Their traits, values, etc. and their ability to deal with conflict, challenges, obstacles, etc. should be considered.

Eilis Lacey

Eilis is a young, naive, vulnerable character who grows and matures over the course of the film. Her youth and open nature make her a likeable character. She copes well in New York when she first arrives, despite her homesickness and sadness, showing her determination and resilience. Her kindness to Father Flood's guests on Christmas Day shows her compassionate, thoughtful nature.

She finds herself torn between two men, but never sets out to selfishly hurt anyone. In fact, it is perhaps her attempts to please and get along with everyone that leads to her finding herself in a relationship with Jim, and so in a situation that she does not know how to resolve.

Her confrontation with Nettles Kelly shows how much she has grown in confidence over the course of the film. She stands up for herself here, which spurs her on to make the decision to return to America and tell her mother the truth about Tony. She takes control of her life, showing determination and maturity.

1. What are your first impressions of Eilis as the film begins?

2. Does your view of Eilis change during the film?
   Give reasons for your answer.

3. Is Eilis cold and calculating or inexperienced and naive in her relationships with men?
   Give reasons for your answer.

4. Is Eilis selfish and cruel in her treatment of Jim and Tony? Is she cowardly to leave the way she does and return to America?

5. Is Eilis a likeable character?
   Give reasons for your answer.
   Is Eilis a relatable character?
   Give reasons for your answer.

6. Is Eilis selfish and self-centred or kind and generous?
   Is she naive and innocent or wise and worldly?
   Refer to the text to support the points you make.

7. What sort of life has Eilis had?
   How has this affected her as a person?

8. Is Eilis faced with a lot of challenges and problems in the film?
How does she deal with these challenges and problems?
What is your response to this?

9. Does Eilis grow and develop over the course of the film?
Give reasons for your answer.

10. Do you like Eilis Lacey?
What makes you feel this way about her?

Selecting Key Moments

The following is a list of key moments from the film.
For each moment, select which mode(s) it belongs to.
Write a short piece outlining what this moment tells you about this mode/
adds to this mode in the film.

- Miss Kelly sacks Eilis when she learns of her plans to go to America.
- Eilis and Rose pack her trunk together.
- Eilis stands on deck, leaving her family behind.
- Eilis is very sick on the way to America.
- Eilis meets Tony's family.
- Father Flood breaks the news of Rose's death.
- Eilis and Tony have sex.
- Eils goes out with Nancy, George and Jim.
- Eilis is offered a job in Davis'.
- Jim asks Eilis to stay in Ireland.

- Miss Kelly reveals that she knows Eilis is married.

- Eilis tells her mother she is leaving.

- Eilis is reunited with Tony.

The Comparative Study: Comparing Texts

Use the following questions to compare your texts, noting the similarities and differences between them. Include examples to support the points that you make.

Cultural Context/Social Setting

Consider each of your chosen texts in your answers.

1. In which of the texts you have studied for the Comparative Study do characters have the most freedom and choice?
   Why is this the case?
   Justify your answer with examples from your chosen texts.

2. In which of your texts are characters most controlled?

3. Who holds the power in each world?
   Who is powerless?

4. In which world is difference most accepted and respected?
   In which world is difference least accepted and respected?

5. Which world is the least tolerant?
   Which world is the most tolerant?
   Include examples to explain your view.

6. Which world is the best to live in if you are a woman?
   Give reasons for your answer.

7. Which world is the best to live in if you are a man?
   Give reasons for your answer.

8. Which world is the best to live in if you are a child?
   Give reasons for your answer.

9. Which text portrays the most violent and volatile world?

10. Which of your texts portrays the safest, most secure place?

11. Which of your texts portrays the most supportive world?

12. Which of these worlds is the darkest, most fearful place?

13. Which of these worlds is the brightest, most joyful place?

14. Which of these places is the most unpredictable?

15. Which text portrays the most traditional world?

16. Which of these societies holds family in the highest esteem?

17. Which of these societies holds love in the highest esteem?
    Which of these societies holds love in the lowest esteem?

18. Which of these societies holds religion in the highest esteem?
    Which of these societies holds religion in the lowest esteem?

19. Which of these societies holds power in the highest esteem?

20. Which of these societies holds wealth in the highest esteem?

21. Where do you see the best treatment of the vulnerable of society? Include examples to support your view.

22. Where do you see the worst treatment of the vulnerable of society? Include examples to support your view.

23. Which of the worlds you have studied is the most materialistic?
    Which of the worlds you have studied is the least materialistic?
    What makes characters have these outlooks?

24. Which of the worlds you have studied is the most secretive?
    What makes characters behave this way?

25. Which of your texts displays the greediest world?
    What makes characters have this attitude?

26. Where is love most important?
    Where is love most successful?

Where is love least important?
Where is love least succesful?
Compare the success of love in each of your chosen texts.
What does this tell you about the worlds of these texts and characters' lives?

27. Which of these worlds appealed to you most?
Give reasons for your answer.

28. Which of these worlds appealed to you least?
Explain your point of view.

29. Which of your texts is home to the most religious or spiritual world?

30. Which of your texts showed the least religious or spiritual society?

31. How important is social class in each of your texts?

32. In which of your texts are characters most accepting of their world and society?

33. In which of your texts do characters challenge their world, society and values most?

34. In which of your texts do you see the greatest inequality?

35. In which of your texts do you see the greatest injustice?

36. Where do characters behave the best towards one another?

How does Cultural Context/Social Setting influence their behaviour?

37. How do characters reflect the Cultural Context/Social Setting of their worlds?
Explain, including examples.

38. How does the Cultural Context/Social Setting of your texts lead to problems and difficulties for the texts' characters?
How does it affect characters' responses to these difficulties?

39. Which key moments best capture the Cultural Context/Social Setting of each of your texts?

40. What similarities do you notice in the Cultural Context/Social Setting of this text and your other Comparative Study texts?

41. What differences do you notice in the Cultural Context/Social Setting of this text and your other Comparative Study texts?

Literary Genre

1. Did you like the way this story was told more than your other Comparative Study texts?
   State what you enjoyed most (and least) about each.

2. Is this text more exciting than your other texts?
   Consider tension, suspense, pacing, conflict and the author's use of the unexpected.

3. How does the author make use of tension in each of your chosen texts?
   Where is it most effective?
   Where is it least effective?
   Use examples to support your point of view.

4. How does the author make use of climax in each of your chosen texts?
   Where is it most effective?
   Where is it least effective?
   Use examples to support your point of view.

5. How does the author make use of resolution in each of your chosen texts?
   Where is it most effective?
   Where is it least effective?
   Use examples to support your point of view.

6. Are characters more engaging in this text than in your other texts?
Refer to each of your texts in your answer.

7. How does the author create vivid, memorable characters in each of your chosen texts?

8. In which of your texts are characters most life-like and compelling?
In which text are characters least life-like and most difficult to relate to?
Refer to each of your texts in your answer.

9. Is the setting more effective in telling the story in this text, than in your other texts?

10. Is this text more unpredictable than your other texts?
Refer to each of your texts in your answer.

11. Does this text have greater emotional power than your other texts?
Was this emotional power created in a more interesting way here or in a different text?
Refer to each of your texts in your answer.

12. What was your favourite literary technique, used by the author of each of your texts?
How did the use of this technique help the storytelling?

13. To what extent are you influenced by the point of view that this story is told from?
Are you influenced to a greater or lesser degree by the

point of view utilised in your other Comparative Study texts?

14. Which key moments best capture Literary Genre in each of your texts?

15. What similarities do you notice in the Literary Genre of this text and your other Comparative Study texts? Mention specific aspects of narrative.

16. What differences do you notice in the Literary Genre of this text and your other Comparative Study texts? Mention specific aspects of narrative.

General Vision and Viewpoint

1. Is life happier and fuller for characters in this text than in your other Comparative Study texts?
Explain your point of view fully.

2. Do characters in this text face more obstacles and difficulties than in your other texts?
Who struggles most?

3. Are characters in this text rewarded more for their struggles than in your other texts?
Do they overcome adversity and achieve true happiness and contentment in a way that is not realised in your other texts?

4. How do events in these texts, and your personal response to these events, help your understanding of the General Vision and Viewpoint of these texts?
Include specific examples in your answer.

5. How does your attitude to central characters help shape your understanding of the General Vision and Viewpoint of your chosen texts?
Include specific reference to your chosen characters in your answer.

6. What aspects of this text did you respond to emotionally? How does this help your understanding of the General Vision and Viewpoint of the text?
How does this compare to your other texts?

7. Is this the brightest, most hopeful and triumphant text you have studied?
Explain why its message is more or less positive than in your other texts.

8. Which of your chosen texts was the bleakest and most upsetting or depressing?
Explain what made it more negative than your other texts. What made them more positive?

9. Plot your three texts on a scale of one to ten from darkest (most pessimistic) to brightest (most optimistic). Add a note to explain their positions.

10. Which key moments best capture the General Vision and Viewpoint of each of your texts?

11. What similarities do you notice in the General Vision and Viewpoint of this text and your other Comparative Study texts?

12. What differences do you notice in the General Vision and Viewpoint of this text and your other Comparative Study texts?

13. Can you relate any aspect of this text to your own life experience?
    If so, how does this help to shape your understanding of the General Vision and Viewpoint of this text?

Theme/Issue - Relationships

1. Are relationships in this text more positive and supportive than the relationships in your other chosen texts?
   Include specific examples in your answer.

2. Rank the relationships you have studied in your various texts from most positive (score of 10) to most negative (score of 1).
   Add a note explaining your choices.

3. Are relationships in this text the most engaging and interesting that you have studied?
   Explain your choice.

4. Rank the relationships you have studied in your various texts from the most interesting (score of 10) to the least interesting (score of 1).
   Add a note explaining your choices.

5. Did you learn most about the theme of relationships from this text or another text on your Comparative Study course?
   Refer to your chosen texts to support your answer.

6. What similarities do you notice in the theme of relationships in this text and your other Comparative Study texts?

7. What differences do you notice in the theme of relationships in this text and your other Comparative Study texts?

8. How do the events of the text impact on the characters' relationships with one another in this text and your other chosen texts?
   Who is most affected?
   Who is least affected?

9. How does conflict impact on the relationships of characters in this text and your other chosen texts?
   Who is most affected?
   Who is least affected?

10. How does social class impact on the relationships of characters in this text and your other chosen texts?

Who is most affected?
Who is least affected?

11. Is the theme of relationships portrayed in an idealistic or realistic way in each of your chosen texts?

12. Did any aspect of the theme of relationships shock or surprise you in your three chosen texts?
Use examples from your texts to support the points that you make.

13. What are the most interesting aspects of the theme of relationships in each of your chosen texts?

14. Which text taught you most about relationships?
Refer to each text in your answer.

15. Which key moments best capture the theme of relationships in each of your texts?

16. What similarities do you notice in the theme of relationships in this text and your other Comparative Study texts?

17. What differences do you notice in the theme of relationships in this text and your other Comparative Study texts?

Hero/Heroine/Villain

Consider the following list of questions for a central character in each of your chosen texts.

1. Who is the most interesting character in the text?
   What makes them interesting?
   What do you like about them?
   What do you dislike about them?
   What are this character's strengths?
   What are this character's weaknesses?

2. How does this character cope with conflict?

3. How does this character cope with the unexpected?

4. Are they a resourceful character?

5. Are they an emotional character?
   Use examples to support your view.

6. Do you empathise with this character? Why/why not?

7. What do you admire about this character?

8. How well does this character relate to and interact with other characters?
   Include examples to support your points.

9. Is this character happy or sad?

10. Are they an active or passive character?
    How do they contribute to the action and storyline of the text?
    Are they important to the story's plot and development?

11. Is this character a good (successful and interesting) main character?

12. Would you like to meet this character?
    If you met them, what would you talk about?

13. If you had any advice for this character, what would it be?

14. Does this character make the story more exciting?
    In what way do they do this?

15. Is this character a hero/heroine or a villain?
    Explain your choice.

16. Identify the key moments in the text that illustrate your chosen character's personality traits/character.

17. On a scale of one to ten (with one being extremely heroic and ten being an evil villain), where would you place your chosen character?
    Give reasons for your choice.
    Where would you place the main characters from your other texts?
    Why would you place them here?

18. Which of your chosen characters do you like and admire most?

What makes them your favourite character?
Give reasons for your answer.

19. Which of your chosen characters do you dislike most?
Explain why you like some more than others.

20. Which of your chosen characters shocked you most?
Give reasons for your answer.

21. Which of your chosen characters impressed you most?
Give reasons for your answer.

22. Which of your chosen characters did you feel most sorry for?
Give reasons for your answer.

23. Who is the most resourceful character you have come across?
Give reasons for your answer.

24. Which of your chosen characters faced the most problems and difficulties?
Did they cope well with these problems?

25. How is your favourite character similar to the characters in your other texts?

26. How is your favourite character different to the characters in your other texts?

27. Choose key moments from each of your texts to highlight your characters' strengths and weaknesses.

www.ingramcontent.com/pod-product-compliance
Lightning Source LLC
Chambersburg PA
CBHW071454080526
44587CB00014B/2106